Editor:
Dona Herweck Rice

Editor-in-Chief:
Sharon Coan, M.S. Ed.

Illustrator:
Wendy Chang

Cover Artist:
Keith Vasconcelles

Art Director:
Elayne Roberts

Product Manager:
Phil Garcia

Imaging:
Alfred Lau

Publishers:
Rachelle Cracchiolo, M.S. Ed.
Mary Dupuy Smith, M.S. Ed.

Interdisciplinary Unit
Survival
CHALLENGING

Author:

Susan Onion

Teacher Created Materials

Teacher Created Materials, Inc.
P.O. Box 1040
Huntington Beach, CA 92647
ISBN-1-55734-604-6

©*1995 Teacher Created Materials, Inc.*   Made in U.S.A.

Perma-Bound

Table of Contents

Introduction

Many of us take our daily survival needs for granted. It is not until we are in a time of need that we remember the importance of a dependable shelter, nutritious food, clean water, adequate clothing, and companionship. We sometimes forget that without these necessities, survival would be a difficult or nearly impossible task.

This unit emphasizes survival in four major settings: wilderness, Arctic, island, and war. For each setting, lessons are planned to extend the theme through a cross-curricular approach. Two literature selections provide a foundation for each series of lessons. An introductory section provides activities which are universal to all four survival settings and can be incorporated into your unit at any time. Suggestions for bulletin boards, class awards, and culminating activities are also included. Each section is also preceded by a division page which may be used on bulletin board displays, as report covers, or other ways which may be beneficial to you and your class.

As a teacher in a self-contained classroom, you will find activities to meet all your curricular needs. As a content area teacher, you may wish to cooperate with your teaching team and introduce the theme together. Although the lessons prepared in this unit are categorized by content areas, you will find that many of the activities are designed to overlap into more than one curricular area.

Survival Book Reviews

Set up a book review board in your room. Choose a bulletin board in your classroom that the students can easily reach to write comments. After each student has read a survival story, he or she can complete a book review card and add it to the board. Use copies of the card at the bottom of this page for this purpose. As other students read the same stories, they can add their own comments to the review card. Peer recommendation will likely prove an excellent way to promote books to your students. An additional bonus will be the insights you gain from your students' opinions.

Below is a brief bibliography of survival stories to share with your students.

Burnford, Sheila. *The Incredible Journey.* (Bantam Books, 1961)
Clark, Mavis Thorpe. *Wildfire.* (Macmillan, 1974)
Cleaver, Vera and Bill. *Where the Lilies Bloom.* (J. B. Lippincott Co., 1969)
Defoe, Daniel. *Robinson Crusoe.* (Watermill Press, 1980)
Fendler, Donn and Egan, Joseph B. *Lost on a Mountain in Maine.* (Beech Tree Books, 1992)
Filipovic, Zlata. *Zlata's Diary: A Child's Life in Sarajevo.* (Viking Penguin, 1994)
Fox, Paula. *The Slave Dancer.* (Dell, 1973)
Frank, Anne. *The Diary of a Young Girl.* (Doubleday, 1967)
George, Jean Craighead. *Julie of the Wolves.* (Harper & Row, Publishers, 1972)
George, Jean Craighead. *My Side of the Mountain.* (E.P. Dutton, 1959)
Hesse, Karen. *Letters from Rifka.* (Puffin Books, 1993)
Holman, Felice. *Slake's Limbo.* (Charles Scribner's Sons, 1974)
Kerr, Judith. *When Hitler Stole Pink Rabbit.* (Coward-CM Cann, 1971)
Kherdian, David. *The Road from Home: The Story of an Armenian Girl.* (Morrow, 1979)
London, Jack. *The Call of the Wild.* (Watermill Press, 1980)
Moeri, Louise. *Save Queen of Sheba.* (E. P. Dutton, 1981)
Morey, Walt. *Canyon Winter.* (E.P. Dutton, 1972)
O'Dell, Scott. *Island of the Blue Dolphins.* (Dell Publishing, 1960)
Paulsen, Gary. *Hatchet.* (Bradbury Press, 1974)
Roth, Arthur. *Iceberg Hermit.* (Four Winds Press, 1974)
Speare, Elizabeth George. *The Sign of the Beaver.* (Dell Publishing, 1983)
Sperry, Armstrong. *Call It Courage.* (Macmillan Publishing Co., 1940)
Taylor, Mildred. *Roll of Thunder Hear My Cry.* (Dial Press, 1977)
Taylor, Theodore. *The Cay.* (Doubleday and Co., 1969)
Truss, Jan. *Jasmine.* (Atheneum, 1982)
Turnbull, Ann. *Maroo of the Winter Caves.* (Clarion Books, 1984)
Wyss, Johann. *The Swiss Family Robinson.* (Macmillan Co., 1926)
Yolen, Jane. *The Devil's Arithmetic.* (Viking Penguin, 1988)

Title:		
Author:		
Name	**Date**	**Comments**

4

Bulletin Board Ideas

Backgrounds: Cover the board with topographic maps, wrapping paper with a tree design, mountain posters, animal footprints, or a map of the world.

Borders: Border the bulletin board with rope, dried or artificial leaves, photographs or drawings of animal footprints, sticks and twigs, paper or plastic icicles, or compasses.

Survival Brainstorm: Following the brainstorming activity about what survival is (page 6), have students prepare a bulletin board with a collage of their ideas.

Survival in Different Settings: Divide a board into quadrants. Label each quadrant with a different setting: *Wilderness, Island, Arctic,* and *War.* Have the students fill in the quadrants with pictures of shelters, foods, clothing, and water sources that are appropriate for or correspond to survival in each of these settings.

Not Knots!: Enlarge the pictures and directions for making knots (pages 104–105). Post these on a bulletin board. Securely attach lightweight rope to the board. Make the board an interactive learning center by having the students practice knotting at this board.

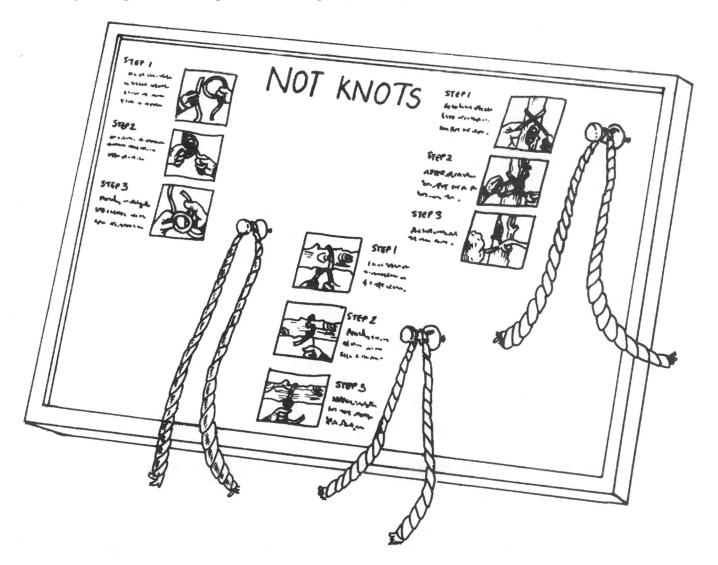

What Is Survival?

Although we all have the same basic needs for physical survival, some of these needs may become more or less important, depending upon the situation. The word survival can be applied to a variety of circumstances. Animals survive daily in the wilderness, families survive under harsh conditions as victims of war, people survive who become lost or stranded in unfamiliar environments, and children survive daily in unsafe city streets. Depending upon an individual's location or needs, survival may take on very different meanings.

For this activity, you will be exploring and expanding your concept of survival. You will need to work in cooperative teams. Once in your teams, work together to brainstorm for a list of ideas, words, and phrases that represent survival. Be sure that everyone in the group contributes some ideas to the list.

When you are finished, share your team's ideas by listing them on the board for a full class discussion. Try to group your ideas by developing category titles such as wilderness, city, animals, foods, etc. This will help organize your thoughts and may contribute to interesting discussions.

Survival Brainstorm

_____   _____

_____   _____

_____   _____

_____   _____

_____   _____

_____   _____

_____   _____

_____   _____

_____   _____

_____   _____

_____   _____

_____   _____

_____   _____

_____   _____

Universal Survival

Name_____

Survival Priorities

When you are lost or stranded, there are several survival priorities that you should keep in mind. All of the priorities are important, but when faced with a severe emergency situation, some of the priorities become more important than others.

Rank the following list in order of importance. After you have decided upon a sequence, explain your reasons for the order. Are there any survival situations in which you might change your ranking? If so, what situations are they, and how would they change the ranking?

- shelter
- fire
- signaling for help
- positive attitude
- water
- first aid
- food

1. _____   _____

                                  _____

2. _____   _____

                                  _____

3. _____   _____

                                  _____

4. _____   _____

                                  _____

5. _____   _____

                                  _____

6. _____   _____

                                  _____

7. _____   _____

                                  _____

Name_____

Survival Scramble

The words scrambled below all have something to do with survival. Unscramble the words. Then, match the numbered letters to the numbered spaces to complete the statement.

1. restelh   ___ ___ ___ ___ ___ ___
                            7

2. tinscint   ___ ___ ___ ___ ___ ___ ___ ___
                                          1

3. drappere   ___ ___ ___ ___ ___ ___ ___ ___
                              5

4. treaw   ___ ___ ___ ___ ___
                         4

5. verysu   ___ ___ ___ ___ ___ ___
              3

6. odof   ___ ___ ___ ___
           2

7. glictonh   ___ ___ ___ ___ ___ ___ ___
                                 6

A person must have ___ ___ ___ ___ ___ ___ ___ for survival.
                     1   2   3   4   5   6   7

Name_____

Character Growth

Most people grow or change during a survival situation. They learn about themselves and develop new skills to meet their challenges. Think about how the characters in the stories we read develop as a result of their experiences. How do they change? What events occur to make them change?

Choose a character. Write five traits that describe the character before his or her survival experience and then write five new traits that describe the character after his or her experience. In the final box, describe the events that brought about these changes in the character.

Character _____

Before	After	Event
1.		
2.		
3.		
4.		
5.		

Story Starters

Outline your primary survival concerns. Then, read one of the following survival scenarios. Write a story to respond to the situation.

Note to the teacher: Students can work individually or in cooperative teams to create their stories.

1. Imagine that you are hiking with a group of friends in the woods of Maine, and the weather changes unpredictably. The rain is falling in sheets, and it is difficult to see where you are going. You decide that you need to find shelter, so you dash into a nearby cave. Once inside, you notice that one of your friends is missing. The storm is still very strong, and it is beginning to get dark. What do you do?

2. You are on a trip with your family in the South Pacific. One day while walking on the beach, you discover an old rowboat. You do not think that anyone will mind if you borrow it for a short time, so you get in and begin to row out into the lagoon. As you reach the edge of the lagoon, a current begins to pull your boat into the ocean. You try to row back, but the current is too strong. Before long, you can no longer see land. What do you do?

3. You are visiting a cousin. Your cousin lives in New York in the Catskill Mountains. It is late December, and there is approximately one foot (30 cm) of snow on the ground. You decide to go hiking in the mountains for the afternoon. Your cousin knows the area well and leads you into an area of the mountains where you have never been. You stop to rest for a minute, and when you turn around, your cousin is gone. You know that your cousin enjoys playing jokes, so you wait for your cousin to return. It is getting late, and your cousin is still nowhere to be found. You have a light pack with some dried fruit and water, but you have no flashlight. You know that it will get dark before you are able to retrace your path in the snow. What do you do?

4. You are skiing with some friends in the Rocky Mountains. It is early spring, and there has been a great deal of snow melting on the upper slopes. As you are traversing across the slopes, you hear a low rumbling in the distance. You see a small cabin nearby, and you and your friends are able to ski over quickly and run into the building. The rumbling increases to a deafening roar as snow crashes down all around you. The cabin remains intact, yet everything is dark. You locate the door but are unable to open it. The windows all appear to be covered with snow. You hear one of your friends moaning in the corner, but you cannot see what is wrong. What do you do?

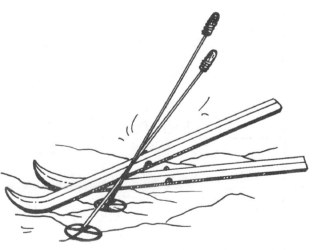

Research Ideas

1. **Animal Survival:** Choose a wild animal and research the special survival techniques it depends upon in the wilderness. How might survival conditions change with the seasons?

2. **Shelters:** Research different styles of shelters and how they are built. Find out what materials they are made of and in what climates they are most useful.

3. **Food:** Find out what wild foods can be found in your area of the country. Where would you find these foods? At what time of the year would you find them? How would you prepare them?

4. **Water:** Research your town's water system. What is the source? How is it purified? Is your town prepared to supply water in an emergency situation?

5. **Nutrition:** Study what nutrients our bodies need to survive and what foods provide good sources of these nutrients.

6. **Fire:** Research different fire-building techniques. What resources are available that you might be able to use if you do not have matches? How can someone build a fire in the wilderness when it is raining?

7. **Navigation:** Research how people are able to find their ways without a compass. How accurate are these other techniques? Are any of them being used by people today?

8. **Survivors:** Research one of the following survivors or choose another survivor you know. What situation did the person survive and how?

    - Anne Frank
    - Helen Keller
    - Robert E. Peary
    - Huynh Quang Nhuong
    - Nelson Mandela

12

Name_____

Water

Our bodies can survive for weeks or even months without food, but we can survive only a few days without water. Our bodies are made of about 60% water. Water is a part of our cells, sweat, tears, and blood. Water helps us process food, build new cells, and regulate our body temperatures. By sweating, we release heat and keep our bodies cooler. If we did not have enough water, we would overheat, and our bodies would not be able to continue their normal functions.

We need between six and eight glasses of water each day to keep our bodies healthy. If we are exercising or are in a very warm climate, we may need more water to replace the fluids that are lost in sweat. This water can come from the fluids we drink as well as some of the foods we eat.

Use the information above and reference books to respond to the following:

1. What are some foods you know that are high in water content?

   _____

   _____

   _____

   _____

   _____

   _____

2. In cases of severe dehydration, such as the dehydration that can occur without water in the desert or on the ocean, one should not eat foods such as bread or meat. Explain why this is true.

   _____

   _____

   _____

   _____

   _____

   _____

3. Try this experiment to see how plants contain water:

   Place a plastic bag over the leaf of a living house plant. Secure a rubber band around the leaf stem at the opening of the plastic bag. After about an hour, what has happened?

Name_____

Food

Food is imperative to survival. Without food, our bodies would not receive the nutrients necessary to perform their natural functions. In dire survival situations, the body can continue for several days without food. But remember, the longer the body goes without food, the weaker it becomes and the less energy it has to survive.

The nutrients in food can be categorized into six groups: carbohydrates, fats, proteins, water, vitamins, and minerals. All of these nutrients work together to help our bodies grow and repair themselves. Most foods are made up of a combination of more than one nutrient. For example, carrots contain carbohydrates, water, protein, vitamins, and minerals. Read the nutritional facts labels on the sides of boxes and cans to find out which nutrients make up some of your favorite foods.

We measure the energy that we gain from our food in calories. For every gram of carbohydrate or protein, we gain four calories. For every gram of fat, we gain nine calories. Water, vitamins, and minerals do not provide any calories. If the body does not use all of the energy provided by the calories, it stores the excess. The result is body fat, and too much fat is unhealthy. As long as you do not eat foods that contain more calories than your body can burn, you do not need to worry about gaining fat.

Collect samples of different cereal boxes. Look at the nutritional facts labels and compare the caloric amounts. (You may simply go to the market and read the labels there.) Also, note the fat contents. The Food and Drug Administration recommends that our daily diets not exceed a total of 30% fat. Given that information, answer the following:

1. Which cereals offer the healthiest meals?

   _____

   _____

   _____

   _____

   _____

2. Which offer the unhealthiest meals?

   _____

   _____

   _____

   _____

   _____

Name_____

Survival Setting

Our survival needs change depending upon our situations. Think about the four survival settings below. Which concerns are unique to each setting? What concerns are the same? Use the diagram to organize your thinking. Then choose the setting that you feel would be the most difficult in which to live. On the back of this paper, explain your reasoning.

Wilderness

Island

All

War

Arctic

Name_____

Remain Calm!

When faced with a severe survival situation, the most important rule to remember is to stay calm. It is easy to panic and to make mistakes which may cost you your life. By staying calm, you will be able to think about your situation and form a clear plan of action.

We all have different ways of coping with fear and stress. Some people find it soothing to sing, while others find it relaxing if they sit quietly for a few minutes or count to ten. It is important that you do whatever works best for you to maintain calm under the circumstances.

List the things that you do or could do to calm yourself before an important test or sports event.

_____

_____

_____

_____

_____

_____

_____

_____

_____

_____

_____

_____

_____

_____

_____

_____

_____

_____

Share your ideas with the class. Add to your list any ideas they have that you had not thought of.

Now, star the three ideas that you think will be of the most benefit to you. Try them yourself for one week. Then, on the back of this paper write a paragraph or two explaining the effects they have had.

Name_____

Navigation

There are four standard principles of navigation. Each principle has its strengths and weaknesses.

Dead Reckoning: This principle is a process of estimating your position based on the direction and rate you have traveled over a period of time. If a map is available, you can plot your course as you travel. If no map of the region is available, you can plot your course on a sheet of blank paper to monitor your progress to a known location.

Celestial: This principle is based on the moon, stars, and planets as they appear in relationship to the earth. Navigators observe the movements of the bodies in the sky and base their navigation on their relative locations.

Electronic: This principle uses electronic instruments to monitor position and bearings. In the case of a ship, electronic equipment is also used to monitor water depths.

Piloting: This principle is usually applied when discussing river navigation. It involves observing geographic landmarks to assess location.

List the pros and cons of each of these navigational principles. Can you think of any situation in which one or more of these principles might be ineffective?

	Pros	**Cons**	**Ineffective**
Dead Reckoning			
Celestial			
Electronic			
Piloting			

Name _____

Rationing

Rationing food and supplies is necessary in a survival emergency. Read the survival scenario and fill in the chart below.

Survival Scenario

Three women are stranded in a storm. They have 12 eggs, 25 sandwiches, 6 candy bars, 3 bags of chips, 13 bagels, 9 oranges, 4 apples, and 7 gallons of drinking water. They know that it will be three days before help can arrive. One of the victims is pregnant and needs one and one-half times more food than anyone else.

Divide the supplies among the victims so each person has her fair share. Use the algebraic formula below to help you solve this problem.

x	=	food share for 1 woman (non-pregnant)
$2x + 1.5x$	=	(total amount of food)
$3.5x$	=	(total amount of food)
$3.5x/3.5$	=	(total amount of food)/3.5
x	=	(total amount of food)/3.5

Divide x by 2 and add that result to x to solve for the pregnant woman. The equation is

$x + x/2$	=	food share for 1 woman (pregnant)

Here is an example using the total number of eggs.

$2x + 1.5x$	=	12
$3.5x$	=	12
$3.5x/3.5$	=	12/3.5
x	=	3.43 (the total number of eggs for 1 non-pregnant woman)
$x + x/2$	=	5.14 (the total number of eggs for the pregnant woman)

person	eggs	sandwiches	candy	chips	bagels	oranges	apples	water
woman 1	3.43							
woman 2	3.43							
pregnant woman	5.14							

Challenge: How much of each food should each woman eat daily?

Shelters

A shelter is necessary for survival. Whether it is a cave, a tent, an alley, or a house, a shelter provides protection from the environment and offers a safe, dry place to store supplies. The type of shelter a person chooses will depend upon his/her needs. If a person is stranded on an island in the Pacific, he or she will need protection from the sun and rain, while a person who is trapped in a storm on the top of a mountain will need shelter from the snow and wind. How might these two shelters look different?

Instructions for building four different shelters are outlined on this and the next page.

Using materials of your choice, build your own miniature version of one of these shelters. If you choose, you may adapt ideas from each shelter and build your own design. Then answer these questions as if your shelter were a usable size.

1. Where would you use your shelter?

2. Against what types of weather could your shelter protect you?

3. How long do you think you could live in your shelter?

Note: Instead of using a tarp in the designs below and on the next page, bark, tree limbs, or brush can be substituted.

A-Frame

To build an A-frame shelter, you will need 1 long pole, 2 shorter poles, rope, a tarp, and stakes.*

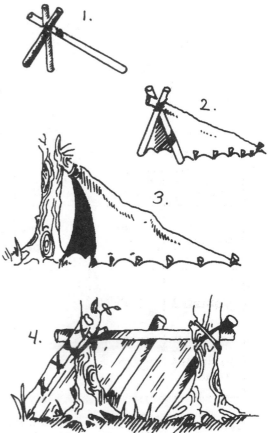

1. Lash the two shorter poles together at the top to make an A shape.

2. Lash the longer pole to the top of the two shorter poles.

3. Balance these poles as shown in figure 1.

4. Attach the tarp to the top of the A shape and drape it over the poles.

5. Use stakes to secure the tarp to the ground as in figure 2.

*(A variation on this shelter can be done with a tree and only one pole. See figure 3.)

Lean-To

To build a lean-to, you will need 2 sturdy trees, at least 4 long poles, rope, stakes, and a tarp.

1. Lash one pole between the 2 trees.

2. Angle the remaining 3 poles along the supporting pole and secure them with rope.

3. Attach the tarp to the top supporting pole and drape it over the three angled poles.

4. Use stakes to secure the tarp to the ground. See figure 4.

Shelters *(cont.)*

Pole Tepee

To build a pole tepee, you will need rope, at least
6 long poles, stakes, and a tarp.

1. Lay three poles on the ground and lash them
   together about 8 inches (20 cm) below the
   top. See figure 5.

2. Set the poles upright in a tripod position.

3. Set and arrange the remaining poles against
   the top of the tripod until you form a circle
   at the base. See figure 6.

4. Tie the top corner of the tarp to the top of
   the tripod. Stretch the tarp around the base
   of the tepee, smoothing and securing it at
   the top and bottom.

5. Tie off the tarp at the front of the tepee,
   leaving a small doorway. See figure 7.

Snow/Sand Wall Shelter

To build a snow or sand wall shelter, you will
need a wall or cave of sand, dirt, or snow, and a
tarp or tree boughs.

1. Dig a hole or trench large enough for your
   body into the wall of snow or dirt.

2. Poke an air vent in the ceiling of the cave.

3. Spread the tarp or boughs over the floor as
   insulation.

4. Block the doorway with more boughs,
   rocks, or snow, leaving a small air vent. See
   figure 8.

Songs of Life and Death

For centuries, music has played an important role in the expression of our feelings about survival. People who are rejoicing about life write songs which reflect their joy, while people who are suffering because of a death write songs which express sorrow.

Read the following Native American songs and write responses explaining what you think the writers were feeling.

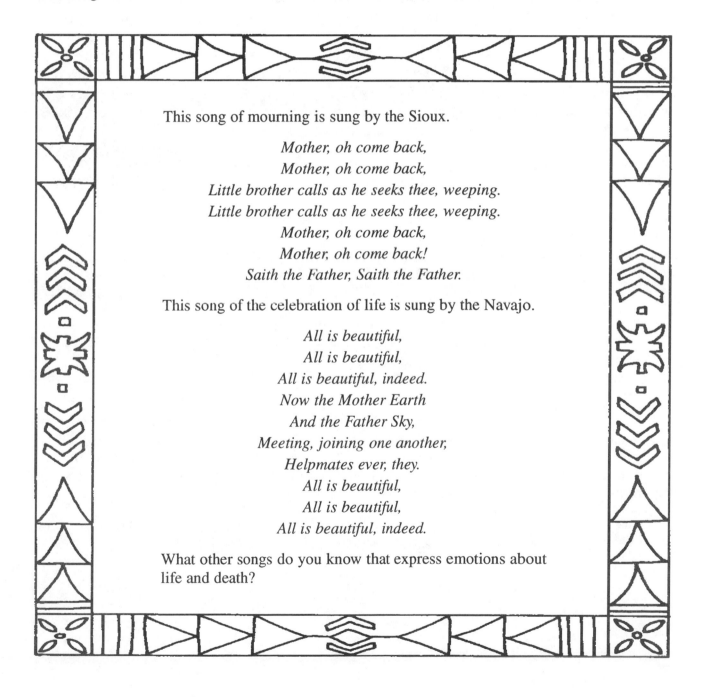

This song of mourning is sung by the Sioux.

Mother, oh come back,
Mother, oh come back,
Little brother calls as he seeks thee, weeping.
Little brother calls as he seeks thee, weeping.
Mother, oh come back,
Mother, oh come back!
Saith the Father, Saith the Father.

This song of the celebration of life is sung by the Navajo.

All is beautiful,
All is beautiful,
All is beautiful, indeed.
Now the Mother Earth
And the Father Sky,
Meeting, joining one another,
Helpmates ever, they.
All is beautiful,
All is beautiful,
All is beautiful, indeed.

What other songs do you know that express emotions about life and death?

Planning a Fitness Program

By keeping yourself in good physical condition, you will have a better chance of surviving in any emergency situation. You can do this by developing a regular fitness program. A good fitness program has several components. Some of these components are regular exercise, a healthy diet, and adequate rest.

Exercise: Exercise strengthens your heart, lungs, and muscles. It also will often improve your mental attitude. Remember a time when you sat at your desk in school all day. How did it feel to get up, stretch, and walk around? Exercise reduces stress and usually feels good. Most people enjoy different forms of exercise. Some people like to run while others would rather do aerobics or play basketball. Of course, some exercises provide a greater workout than others. For example, swimming exerts more energy than walking, but both are good for you. When planning a fitness program, it is best to choose exercises you enjoy so that you will be more likely to stick with the program. It takes only 20–30 minutes for most exercises to provide some benefit.

*Make a list of exercises. Note which ones would provide you with the greatest workout. Then mark the ones which you enjoy.

Healthy Diet: A healthy diet is based on the food pyramid. According to the pyramid, we should eat: 6–11 servings from the bread, cereal, and pasta group, 3–5 servings from the vegetable group, 2–4 servings from the fruit group, 2–3 servings from the milk, cheese, and yogurt group, and 2–3 servings from the meat, poultry, beans, eggs, and nut group. Fats, oils, and sweets should be eaten sparingly. By following this plan for a healthy diet, you will naturally receive the nutrients that your body needs to function.

*Design a week's menus which meet these requirements for a healthy diet. In your menus, try to incorporate the foods that you usually like to eat.

Rest: We all have mornings when we do not want to get out of bed and feel like we could use more sleep. This can be a result of several things. You may have gone to bed late, you may not have slept well, or you may be tired from an exceptionally busy activity on the previous day. It is important to try to schedule an adequate amount of time for sleep. Your body needs time to rest each night so it can recuperate from its exertions during the day. Although sleep needs vary from one individual to the next, most growing bodies need between eight and ten hours of sleep each night.

*Keep a sleep diary for several nights to record the number of hours that you slept and how you felt during the day. This will help you assess how much sleep you need to feel well.

Fitness Schedule

Use the information you gained from the activities on the previous page to help you fill out your own fitness schedule. Fill in the chart with activities that you do during the day. Briefly describe your meals and try to schedule at least one 20–30–minute exercise time each day. Remember to plan for adequate sleep time. While making the chart, also remember to allot times for responsibilities (like homework) and times for pleasure (like watching television).

Time	Sun.	Mon.	Tue.	Wed.	Thu.	Fri.	Sat.

Wilderness Survival

Names _____

Wilderness Preparation

You are preparing to hike in the Maine woods in the month of September. Your trip will take three days and two nights. You have hiked this trail before and are very familiar with the area. The weather is questionable. Your backpack is small, and you have room for only ten items.

Below, you will find a list of several items recommended for backcountry hiking. In cooperative teams, place these items in order of importance. Then, choose the top ten items you will take on your hike. Be prepared to support your choices. You will compare your team's list with other teams' lists and attempt to convince them that your top ten items are the most important.

Top Ten Items

- flashlight
- raingear   1. _____
- map
- compass   2. _____
- food
- first aid kit   3. _____
- matches
- water   4. _____
- extra clothes
- knife   5. _____
- water purifier
- pan   6. _____
- water bottle
- tent   7. _____
- rope
- sleeping bag   8. _____
- silverware
- backpacking stove and fuel   9. _____
- dishes
- trash bag   10. _____

Note to the Teacher: After the teams have completed their lists, regroup the students into new teams. These new team members must present their lists to one another, discuss the lists, and come up with one new list upon which everyone agrees. Team members should then return to their original teams to compare results. To ensure completion, a time limit can be set for each phase of this activity.

Name_____

Tree and Plant Wordsearch

Locate the trees and plants listed below. They may be vertical, horizontal, or diagonal.

aspen	walnut	dogtooth violet	cattail
ash	apple	skunk cabbage	onions
beech	oaks	dandelion	bloodroot
pine	white birch	strawberries	mushrooms
maple	poplar	trillium	blueberry
hemlock	sassafras	arrowleaf	
hickory	willow	water lily	

```
J F U M L S H E N A H S J J H M A P L E S T S J U S M K D
H C V W L T R R X M I A W B H W W B G O I R A N K K O R O
E W Q A A V A K F B C R Y O L H C B M K J I W H T U C B G
M A S M J L L F R B K A R C G I O J T R P L A F V N M J T
L N M K P B N C X Z O A R T C T S A L I I L A N G K C X O
O C D O X V U U S O R Q O D G E N T M K N I G J R C B K O
C X P W I F H T T V Y M D R I B M D R N E U A B T A M W T
K J S D H R F U E J D H F G K I N D G A X M B D T B M I H
C A T T A I L V C S A S S A F R A S M K W S D G H B K L V
S I H U F N H J F J K F E O O C S N H A C B H G F A M L I
A R R O W L E A F D H G K J F H S G B S K L E B G G V O O
D H S J F B L U E B E R R Y K E I T B H L I U R W E S W L
J H D F K G E O I M U S H R O O M S F H F L G H R L R Y E
I O A K S F G E D J H D G J H F G J T E Y D N J I I V G T
S H K K J O O U C G D F D G H G J K L F D D F W T Y E V S
D L S J I W O E R H L T R O D N F P M O N I O N S C D S X
W A T E R L I L Y D J D O T T J P K S D R F K E I R P C I
H J I S F I E U T G I S K F R A L B L O O D R O O T D H G
N A S P E N N F D A N D E L I O N S H R J I O E R J F X K
```

Edible Wild Plants

Most people panic when they become lost in the woods without food and supplies, but with the right knowledge anyone can forage for food and survive. There are thousands of edible plants growing in the wild throughout the world. Some, such as fiddleheads, dandelion greens, and cattails, are regularly harvested by people who consider these wild plants delicacies.

Choose one of the following plants to research. Write a brief description and find a picture of the plant. Then, try to find a recipe in which this plant may be used. There are several cookbooks which base recipes solely on wild plants. Share your information with your class by displaying it on an edible plant bulletin board or table.

- amaranths
- bugleweed
- burdocks
- cattail
- chicory
- clovers
- dandelion
- fiddlehead
- fireweed
- milkweed
- pokeweed

- Queen Anne's lace
- roses
- skunk cabbage
- sorrels
- sunflower
- trillium
- violets
- water lilies
- wild onions
- woundwort

Note: Before eating any wild plant, be absolutely certain that it is the correct plant. Many wild plants look similar to others, and many of them are poisonous.

Name_____

Animal Tracking

Animal tracks can tell you a lot about how an animal survives. By following tracks, you can learn what an animal eats, what its daily routine is, and where it sleeps. By reading animal tracks, you can also learn about which animals may live in an area and how plentiful their herds or families may be.

The following are tracks of some of the animals you may observe in the wilderness. Try to identify the animals by looking at only the tracks.

_____ raccoon   _____ fox   _____ deer   _____ deer mouse

_____ mink   _____ rabbit   _____ skunk   _____ squirrel

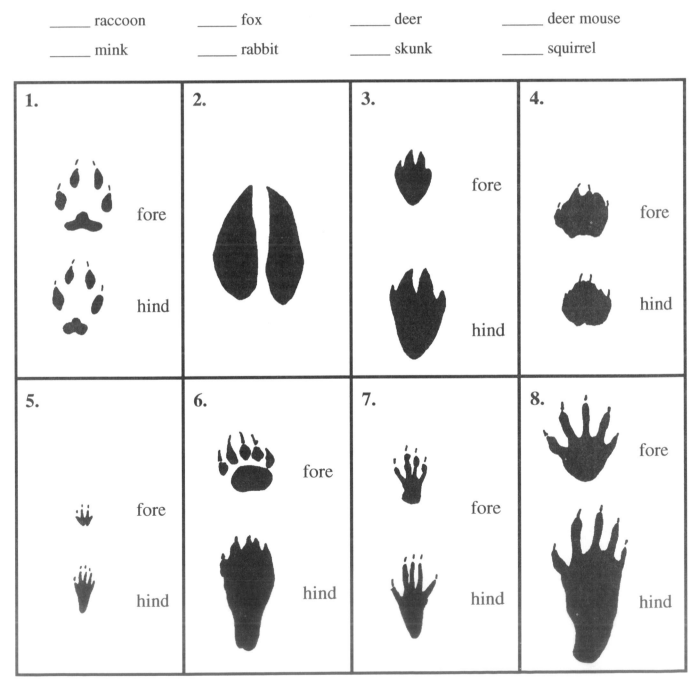

Name_____

Animal Survival Instincts

Every animal behavior occurs as a reaction to some stimulus. This reaction is often based on instinct. Nature has provided animals with an instinctive ability to read signs and to respond in ways that will protect their safety.

Read the animal facts listed below. Work with a partner to match the behaviors with the animals. Then choose one of the animals and write a paragraph explaining how you think the behavior helps this animal survive.

monkey	crow	firefly	bee	kitten
turkey	fawn	swallow	wolf	crocodile

1. This animal swallows its young as soon as they hatch from the nest.   1. _____

2. This animal illuminates its abdomen.   2. _____

3. This animal sprays its scent on trees.   3. _____

4. This animal rubs ants over its body.   4. _____

5. This animal will freeze at the first sign of danger.   5. _____

6. This animal will back away from a high ledge even though it has not experienced heights before.   6. _____

7. This animal has migrated to South America from San Juan Capistrano, California, during the same week in October and returned the same week in March for the last 200 years.   7. _____

8. This animal does not recognize its own young by sight and will kill them if they do not make the right sound.   8. _____

9. This animal dances for its friends.   9. _____

10. This animal smiles at older males of its species.   10. _____

Name _____

Fire Making

To demonstrate how difficult it is to make a fire without matches, set up the following fire starting experiments at the front of the class. Have student volunteers aid you with the demonstrations. Afterwards, ask the students to answer these questions: Which methods were most successful? Do you think you could do this in the wilderness? Would your fire start if your bark and twigs were wet?

Flint and Steel

Materials:
- flint
- steel
- bowl of water
- dry bark or small twigs
- small piece of lint, cloth, or a tissue
- old cookie sheet

Directions:

Place the lint on the cookie sheet. Have a student hold the flint and steel near the lint and strike them together to attempt to make a spark. When a spark lands on the lint and begins to smolder, gently blow on the spark and try to create a flame. Add small pieces of bark or twigs until you have a small fire. Put the fire out with the water. (This is not an easy fire making method, and it may take several tries to make an adequate spark.)

Lens or Mirror

Materials:
- lens, magnifying glass, or mirror
- old cookie sheet
- a small piece of lint, cloth, or tissue
- water
- a sunny day
- dry bark or small twigs

Directions:

You must have a location with direct sunlight to do this experiment. Place the lint on the cookie sheet. Have a student hold the lens and direct the beam of sunlight through the lens and onto the lint. Hold the lens steady until the lint begins to smolder. Gently blow on the lint until a flame begins. Add small pieces of bark or twigs until you have a small fire. Put out the fire with the water.

Two Sticks

Materials:
- knife
- dry bark or twigs
- water
- dry board
- straight, dry stick about ³/₄" (2 cm) thick
- small piece of lint, cloth, or tissue
- old cookie sheet

Directions:

Cut a V-shaped notch in the edge of the board. Then, carve a small dent in the board directly behind the notch. Place the cookie sheet on the floor. Set the board on the cookie sheet with the lint set in the board's notch. Use your feet or knees to hold the board in place. (You may want to sit down.) Take the straight stick, place it in the small dent, and then spin it back and forth between the palms of your hands as fast as you can. Continue spinning the stick until the board begins to smolder. Gently blow on the notch until you see a flame. Add dry bark or twigs to the lint until you have a small fire. Put out the fire with the water. (This is a very tiring and time consuming method for making a fire.)

Names _____

Waterproofing

Some fabrics are better than others at resisting wind and rain. This usually depends upon the number of pores (or openings) in the fabric within a given area. If a fabric has small pores, it tends to be water resistant. If a fabric has larger pores, it tends not to be. Try the experiment below to test the water resistance of some common fabrics.

Materials:

- water bowls
- tablespoons
- stopwatches or watches with second hands
- 1' (30 cm) square pieces of different fabrics (nylon, silk, cotton, rayon, wool, or Gor-tex®)

Experiment:

Divide the class into cooperative teams of five. Two of the team members will hold fabrics, one will pour water, one will time the water as it goes through the fabrics, and one will record the results.

Hold the piece of fabric by the corners so that there is a dip in the center. Measure 1 tablespoon (15 mL) of water and pour it onto the center of the fabric. Time how long it takes for the water to drip through the fabric. Write down any observations.

As an extension, try treating the fabrics with water repellent materials such as silicon spray or beeswax. Does this change your results?

fabric	time	observations
1.		
2.		
3.		
4.		
5.		
6.		

Answer:

Which fabrics were most water resistant? _____

Which fabrics were least water resistant? _____

Name_____

Food Drying

Who Dries Foods?

Sun drying is the oldest, most natural method of drying food. Since the times of the ancient Egyptians and Greeks, people have been drying food as a method of preserving it and extending its use. The early American colonists depended on dried food stores during the long winter months. Food drying was necessary for any family which was self-reliant during the winter. During WWI, the government spent much time and money researching better ways of food drying so they could more efficiently feed their armies in the field. In the 1930s, during the Great Depression, many homemakers resorted to food drying as an inexpensive way to extend the life of their garden fruits and vegetables. During WWII, food drying was again renewed. Today, the United States has many companies that mass produce dried foods. These dried foods are often used today for camping, hiking, or just for a healthy snack.

Why Dried Foods?

Bacteria and molds that spoil foods need moisture, warmth, and air to grow. By drying foods and keeping them dry, the bacteria and molds are unable to grow. This process extends the shelf life of many foods to four to eight months.

Think About It

Answer the questions listed below. Remember to supply a reason for each opinion. Then, share your answers with a partner. Research your answers to see whether you are right.

1. Which foods do you think are the easiest to dry? Why? _____

   _____

2. Which foods do you think are more difficult to dry? Why? _____

   _____

3. There are many ways to preserve foods. Why might drying be the most efficient way of preserving and storing foods for some people? _____

   _____

4. What are some dried foods that you have eaten? Do they taste different when they are not dried? How? _____

5. Do you like these foods better dried? Why or why not? _____

   _____

Extension: Visit a store that sells dried foods. Make a list of these foods and how long their shelf lives are. Compare these foods to foods that are not dried. How must these foods be stored, and how long are their shelf lives?

Food Drying *(cont.)*

Sun Drying Method

You will need five to seven days to sun dry. Follow these steps.

Materials:

- apples
- salt
- blocks
- water
- nylon netting
- airtight plastic container
- self-sealing plastic bags
- clean window screen

Directions:

1. Prepare a sun-drying rack. Take the clean screen and place it on four blocks so it does not touch the ground. Be sure to set your rack in a place that will receive constant sunlight.

2. Core, wash, and peel the apples.

3. Slice the apples into rings or quarter slices. (Quartered slices may take longer to dry.)

4. Pretreat the slices by soaking them in a solution of 4 tablespoons (60 mL) salt to one gallon (3.8 L) of water for ten minutes. (Many fruits will lose their natural colors and flavors if not pretreated. Pretreating fruit will help retain colors and flavors.)

5. Lay fruit on the drying screen in a single layer. After placing the apples on this screen, cover the fruit with a layer of nylon netting. Prop up the netting with two more blocks to prevent it from touching the fruit.

6. Turn the apples 3–4 times a day so the slices will dry evenly. (Be sure to bring the tray inside at night so it will not become damp with dew.)

7. Apples should take four to five days to dry. (This will vary depending upon the humidity in the air.) Check for dryness by gently squeezing the slices. There should be no moisture and the apples should feel leathery.

8. After sun drying the apples, place the slices in an airtight plastic container for 2–3 days. Shake the container once a day. This will help distribute any excess moisture. If there is any moisture forming on the lid of the container, the apples may need to be returned to the sun-drying rack for another day.

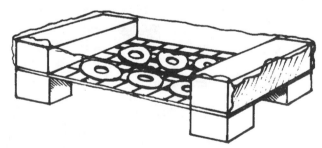

9. Store the finished fruit in small, self-sealing plastic bags.

10. Enjoy eating!

Food Drying (cont.)

Oven Drying Method

You will need five to seven hours to oven dry.   Follow these steps.

Materials:

- apples
- salt
- oven
- water
- cookie cooling rack
- airtight plastic container
- self-sealing plastic bags
- nylon netting/cheese cloth

Directions:

1. Prepare an oven-drying rack. Take the metal cookie cooling rack and cover it with cheese cloth. (By using a cookie rack instead of a flat pan, the fruit will receive more air circulation during the drying process and will dry more evenly.)

2. Core, wash, and peel the apples.

3. Slice the apples into rings or quarter slices. (Quartered slices may take longer to dry.)

4. Pretreat the slices by soaking them in a solution of 4 tablespoons (60 mL) salt to one gallon (3.8 L) of water for ten minutes. (Many fruits will lose their natural colors and flavors if not pretreated. Pretreating the fruit will help retain colors and flavors.)

5. Place the apple slices on the oven-drying rack in a single layer.

6. Turn on the oven to 150°F (70°C).

7. Place the rack in the oven. Be sure to leave the oven door propped open 2–4 inches (5–10 cm). Watch the apples carefully near the end of the drying process. As there is less moisture, less heat is needed for drying.

8. The apples should be dry in 5–7 hours.

9. After drying the apples, place the slices in an airtight plastic container for 2–3 days. Shake the container once a day. This will help distribute any excess moisture. If there is any moisture forming on the lid of the container, the apples may need to be returned to the oven.

10. Store the finished fruit in small, self-sealing plastic bags.

11. Enjoy eating!

Name_____

Nutritional Number Facts

To find out about the nutrients that are important to our diets, solve the problems below. Then write the letter that is beside each answer every time you find it in the puzzle.

25 x 32 = A	824 ÷ 4 = B	47 x 21 = C	765 ÷ 15 = D	14 x 42 = E	78 x 3 = F	864 ÷ 12 = H	63 x 12 = I	29 x 17 = L	594 ÷ 22 = M
55 x 11 = N	356 ÷ 2 = O	17 x 15 = P	792 ÷ 12 = R	600 ÷ 10 = S	25 x 16 = T	27 x 12 = U	19 x 31 = V	380 ÷ 20 = W	52 x 12 = Y

1. These are essential for the growth, development and repair of body tissues. Some good sources of this nutrient are fish, meat, poultry, and eggs.

 __255__ __66__ __178__ __400__ __588__ __756__ __605__ __60__

2. These provide the main source of energy for our bodies. Some good sources of this nutrient are fruits, vegetables, breads, and pasta.

 __987__ __800__ __66__ __206__ __178__ __72__ __624__ __51__ __66__ __800__ __400__ __588__ __60__

3. These provide a source of stored energy and carry vitamins to body cells. They also insulate the body. Some good sources of this nutrient are dairy products, meats, and nuts.

 __234__ __800__ __400__ __60__

4. These nutrients are necessary to regulate chemical reactions in our bodies. They are found in a variety of foods. By eating a well-balanced diet, these nutrients will naturally be consumed in adequate amounts.

 __27__ __756__ __605__ __588__ __66__ __800__ __493__ __60__

5. These promote necessary chemical reactions in our bodies. These nutrients are also found in a variety of foods and will be naturally consumed by eating a well-balanced diet.

 __589__ __756__ __400__ __800__ __27__ __756__ __605__ __60__

6. This nutrient helps digestion, regulates body temperature, and makes up our blood. It is absolutely necessary for survival.

 __19__ __800__ __400__ __588__ __66__

Notch Calendar

Sam does not have a calendar with him in the Catskill Mountains. He keeps track of the dates by cutting notches in sticks.

You can keep your own notch calendar in the classroom. You will need some long, straight sticks and a knife. Cut one new notch in the stick each day. Be sure to cut extra notches on weekends and holidays. When you reach the end of the month, begin a new stick. To find out the date, you only need to count the sticks and notches.

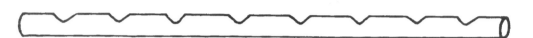

The following two methods might be helpful in remembering how many days are in each month.

Poem

Learn and recite this poem.

> *Thirty days hath September,*
> *April, June, and November.*
> *All the rest have thirty-one*
> *Except for February alone,*
> *Which has twenty-eight days clear*
> *And twenty-nine in each Leap Year.*

Hand

Place your two fists together as shown in the picture. Say the months in order, beginning with your left hand's smallest knuckle. Say a month's name at each knuckle and at each groove between the knuckles. Each knuckle represents a month with 31 days. The groove between each knuckle is a month with fewer than 31 days. Be sure that where your hands meet (July and August) you move from knuckle to knuckle since both July and August have 31 days.

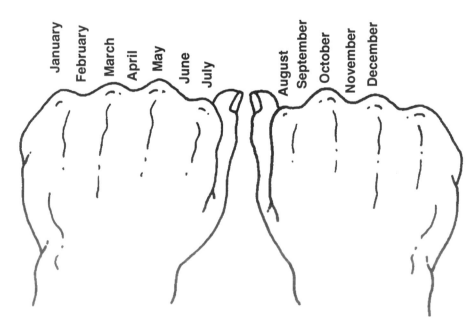

Average Hiking Rate

The average person walks about three miles (5 km) in one hour. Knowing how far you can walk in an hour is a useful piece of information in the wilderness. If you become lost in the woods and you know that you have been walking at a fairly steady pace for 30 minutes, you will be able to calculate about how far you have traveled. Try the activity below to calculate your average walking speed.

If you do not have a track available to you, measure out a quarter mile (half km) loop in the school yard or around a neighboring park. You can clock this distance on a car or bicycle odometer or measure it out by hand. Once you have your course set, time yourself as you begin walking the loop at your normal walking pace. Continue walking the loop for twenty minutes without stopping. Keep track of the number of times you complete the loop. At the end of twenty minutes, mark your stopping location on the loop.

To calculate your walking speed:

Estimate your additional lap distance to the nearest $\frac{1}{4}$ lap. For example, if you walked 2 laps and $\frac{1}{2}$ more, you walked 2.5 laps. Then, multiply the number of laps by 4 (ex.: 2.5 x 4 = 10). Divide your answer by 3 (ex.: 10 ÷ 3 = 3.3 or $3\frac{1}{3}$ miles or kilometers per hour)

You may wish to try this activity more than once and then take the average of the times to find a more accurate walking pace.

Keep in mind that when you are hiking in the wilderness, you may not be on a flat surface. Hiking in the mountains or at a higher elevation will most likely slow your pace. Also, after hiking for three hours, you may become tired and walk more slowly.

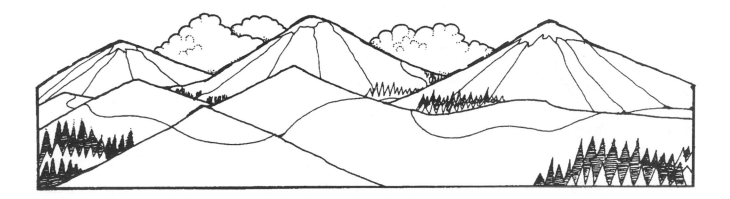

Casting Tracks

Animal tracks can be preserved indefinitely by making a plaster cast of the tracks. Many researchers use this technique to make a permanent record of their findings. The following activity can be an interesting way to explore how animal tracks are made and preserved. If you have an outside location available to you, you might want to try this activity outdoors with authentic tracks. You could have a pet brought in to make tracks or use someone's footprint. Make sure that your track is indented enough in the dirt to give you a good casting.

Materials:

- plaster of Paris
- bowl for mixing
- water
- a track (or source for making a track)
- long strip of cardboard
- clay (for indoor casting)

Directions:

1. Mix the plaster of Paris by following the directions on the bag or box.

2. Shape the cardboard strip into a circle large enough to surround the track. Tape the ends securely together to hold.

3. Place the cardboard circle around the track. Pour the plaster of Paris mixture into the circle and allow it to dry (about 15 minutes).

4. When the cast is dry, pick it up and gently brush off the dirt.

If you do not have an outdoor setting available to you, you can make your own tracks using a clay mold. Have the students use the tracks on page 28 as a model to create their own prints in the clay. The same method of casting described above can be used for these inside molds. Make sure that your cardboard circle is secure around the clay print so that the plaster will not leak.

Extension: After you have made castings of various animal footprints, have your students press the castings into a pan of damp sand to make imprints. Ask students to try to identify the animals that might have made these imprints.

Trail Markers

Trail markers are important to people hiking in the wilderness. If a trail is not well marked, it is easy to become lost.

There are many ways that rangers and guides mark trails in the wilderness. The trail markers that they use usually depend upon the environment and resources available for marking. Some standard trail marking methods are listed below.

Trail heads are often marked with a permanent *sign* which identifies the name of the trail and, sometimes, the distance to the next trail intersection. In rocky areas, a ranger may use *cairns* to mark a trail. These are piles of rocks placed as landmarks along the trail. In a snowy area, a ranger sometimes marks the trail with long *stakes* that have brightly colored ribbons tied to the ends. These are easy to see from a distance and will still show up after a snowfall. In wooded areas, a variety of markers may be used. Trails are often marked with small, brightly colored *paint* marks on rocks and trees. Another method a ranger might use is to tie a brightly colored piece of *cloth* around the limbs of the trees along the trail. Occasionally, a trail will be marked with *knife cuts* in the tree trunks which are then painted.

Activity

Divide the class into teams. Give each team a differently colored piece of chalk to mark their trails. (Chalk is less permanent than paint.) Have the first team mark a trail for another team to follow through the playground or a nearby park. Tell them to place their marks on trees and rocks along their trail. When the first team returns, send out the following team. Have the following team make a map of the first team's trail. Remind students that trail markers should be set frequently enough so that the followers have no questions about where the trail leads. Also, remind them that the trail marks need to be spots only large enough for the followers to notice. They do not need to be a display.

My Side of the Mountain

by Jean Craighead George

(E.P. Dutton, 1959)

(Available in Canada: Penguin; the United Kingdom and Australia: Penguin Ltd.)

Sam Gribley leaves his home in New York City to live on his great-grandfather's land in the Catskill Mountains. He leaves New York in May with only a pen knife, a ball of cord, an ax, flint and steel, and forty dollars. No one believes that he will stay in the wilderness. When he arrives in the mountains, he finds his great-grandfather's land and makes a home in an old hemlock tree. He learns about his environment by observing the animals, doing research in the library, and by undergoing the processes of trial and error. He traps and forages for food, makes his own clothes, and hunts with a pet falcon. When winter comes, he lives on the food that he stored during the summer months. During the year, he meets people lost in the woods who later return to visit him. Through his experiences in the Catskill Mountains, Sam becomes a self-sufficient, resourceful survivor living in the wild.

Name_____

Predictions

When Sam left New York City to live on his great-grandfather's land in the Catskill Mountain wilderness, he took only a few precious items. He carried a penknife, a ball of cord, an ax, flint and steel, and forty dollars in his pockets. What do you think Sam planned to do with these items? Write your predictions on the back.

- penknife
- ball of cord
- ax
- flint and steel
- forty dollars

Do you think Sam was wise when he selected these items to take with him? Explain your answer on the back.

If you were to leave your home to live in the wilderness, what important items would you take? Make a list of the ten most important items. Then, explain why you would choose to take each. Save this list until you have finished reading *My Side of the Mountain*. Then look back at your list to see if you would make any changes.

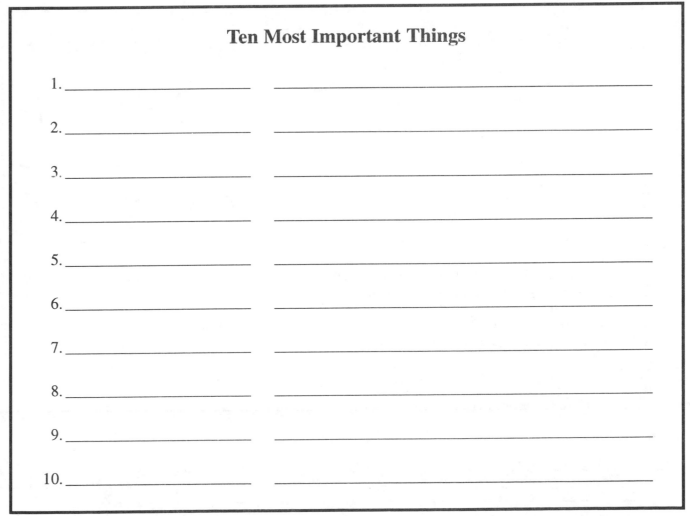

Ten Most Important Things

1. _____ _____

2. _____ _____

3. _____ _____

4. _____ _____

5. _____ _____

6. _____ _____

7. _____ _____

8. _____ _____

9. _____ _____

10. _____ _____

Name_____

Catskills Map

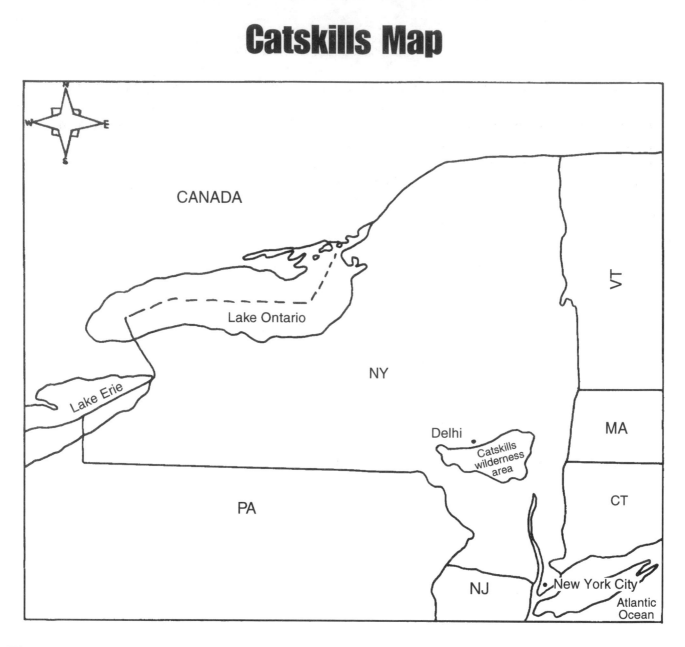

The town of Delhi is about 200 miles (320 km) north of New York City. Sam's great-grandfather's farm was located in the Catskill Mountains near this town.

Would you travel this distance by yourself to a town you had never seen to find your great-grandfather's land? What would you do once you arrived there?

_____

_____

_____

_____

_____

Name_____

Fish Hooks

Sam relies on fish as one of his major sources of food. Fish provides necessary protein and most types of fish are less fatty than red meats. Sam knew that fish would be important to his diet until he learned how to catch other animals. Since Sam did not bring fish hooks with him from New York, he had to make his own hooks from the materials that were available to him in the wilderness. Fortunately, Sam had read about how to make hooks while he was in the library. Read Sam's directions in the second chapter of *My Side of the Mountain*. Following these directions, try to construct your own fish hook. (You might want to use string or thread instead of green bark to hold your hook together.) Once your hook is complete, answer the following questions.

1. What difficulties did you have while making your hook? _____

   _____

   _____

   _____

   _____

   _____

2. Will your hook catch fish? Why or why not? _____

   _____

   _____

   _____

   _____

   _____

   _____

3. Did you discover a better building technique? If you did, outline the directions for your new technique._____

   _____

   _____

   _____

   _____

Name_____

Thoreau

When Bando first meets Sam, he decides to call him "Thoreau." Bando selects the name because Sam reminds him of a man who lived in New England in the 1800s. Henry David Thoreau was a well-known writer, philosopher, and naturalist. Thoreau was born in Concord, Massachusetts, in 1817. He attended Harvard University, and, for a couple of years, went on to teach in a school kept by his brother in Maine. He later lived with and became the protegé of the poet Ralph Waldo Emerson. Some of Thoreau's best known works are *A Week on the Concord and Merrimac Rivers*, *On the Duty of Civil Disobedience*, and *Walden*. Henry David Thoreau wrote *Walden* while living as a recluse in a shack on a small pond in upper-state Massachusetts. During the two years that Thoreau spent in the shack on Walden Pond, he wrote about his relationships with nature and society and his observations of the animals around him. Thoreau is also known for being an independent individual. In 1846, he was sent to jail because he refused to pay a poll tax. He did not want his money to support the Mexican War.

Research to find out more about Henry David Thoreau and his writings. Share your information with the rest of your class. Then, read the following passage from *Walden* in the chapter titled "Winter Animals."

> *Usually the red squirrel waked me in the dawn, coursing over the roof and up and down the sides of the house, as if sent out of the woods for this purpose. In the course of the winter I threw half a bushel of ears of sweet corn which had not got ripe, onto the snow crust by my door, and was amused by watching the motions of the various animals which were baited by it. In the twilight and the night the rabbits came regularly and made a hearty meal. All day long the red squirrel came and went, and afforded me much entertainment by their manoeuvres.*

Answer:

In what ways does this description remind you of Sam?_____

_____

_____

_____

_____

_____

_____

_____

_____

_____

Name_____

Graphing Food

Sam has to plan ahead to store food for the winter months. The graphs below show two ways Sam could have organized his food. Use the graphs to answer the questions.

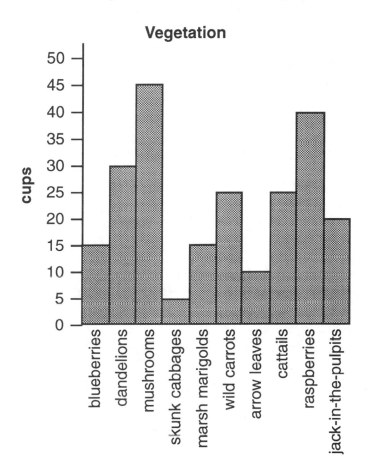

Vegetation

(**hint:** 2 cups = 1 pint; 2 pints = 1 quart)

1. How many cups of cattails does Sam have? _____

2. How many cups of berries are there?_____

3. How many quarts of raspberries have been stored? _____

4. There are ten cups of arrow leaves. How many more cups of dandelions than arrow leaves are there? _____

5. How many pints of jack-in-the-pulpits are there? _____

6. If Sam made bread and used one pint of cattails to make flour, how many cups would he have left? _____

7. Which plant has Sam stored the least amount of? _____

8. Which plant has Sam stored the greatest amount of? _____

9. If Sam ate half his store of wild carrots by January, how many cups would he have left for the spring months? _____

(**hint:** 16 ounces = 1 pound)

1. How many pounds of smoked squirrel are there? _____

2. How many ounces of rabbit meat does Sam have stored? _____

3. How many more pounds of venison than fish are there? _____

4. If Sam used 24 ounces of turtle to make soup, how many pounds would he have left? _____

5. How many pounds of meat does Sam have in all? _____

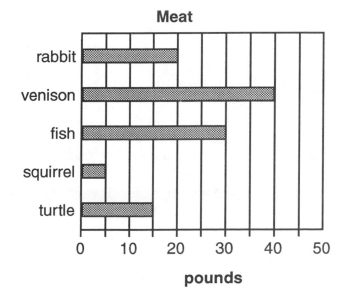

Meat

Name _____

Companionship

Sam lives on the mountain with several wild animals as his neighbors. As Sam spends more time alone in the wilderness without human contact, he begins to name his neighbors. How does naming the animals help Sam? What does this tell us about Sam's character?

Read the animal names listed below. Identify the animals and explain why Sam chooses each name.

1. Frightful _____

   _____

2. The Baron _____

   _____

3. Jessie C. James _____

   _____

4. Mr. Bracket _____

   _____

5. Mrs. O'Brien _____

   _____

6. Mrs. Callaway _____

   _____

7. Mrs. Federio _____

   _____

8. Barometer _____

   _____

Based on Sam's descriptions, do you think the names are appropriate? Explain.

_____

_____

_____

_____

Name_____

Math in the Catskills

The quotes for the math problems below are all taken from *My Side of the Mountain*. Solve the problems and then make up some of your own to share with the class.

1. "Five notches into June, my house was done. I could stand in it, lie down in it, and there was room left over for a stump to sit on."

   a. If Sam is 5' 2" (1.55 m) tall, how many inches (cm) long does he have to cut the inside of his tree?

   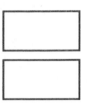

   b. The Hemlock tree is 6' (1.8 m) in diameter. How thick are Sam's walls?

2. "That's the best strawberry patch in the entire Catskill range. I come up here every spring. For forty years I've come to that meadow for my strawberries."

   a. If Mrs. Fielder walked to the patch three times each spring and picked 2 quarts (1.9 liters) of strawberries each time, how many quarts (liters) of berries would she pick in forty years?

   b. If she made jelly with this year's berries, and she needed one cup (250 mL) of strawberries for each jar, how many jars could she make?

3. "I left New York in May."

   a. If Sam left the city on May 16, and he has 68 notches in his calendar sticks, what is the date?

   b. How many notches would he have on his sticks on Thanksgiving day?

4. "When I first walked in these shoes, I tripped on my toes and fell, but at the end of the first day I could walk from the tree to the gorge in half the time."

   a. If it took Sam 1 ½ hours to walk to the gorge without snowshoes, how long would it take him to walk the distance with snowshoes?

   b. If it is two miles (3.2 km) to the gorge, how far can Sam walk in snowshoes in four hours?

Name_____

Modern Conveniences

Sam's life in the mountains is extremely difficult. He learns very early that he has to plan ahead and prepare for everything. In the beginning, Sam spends every waking moment foraging or hunting for food, carrying water, building a shelter, preparing fires, or planning for his future survival. Since Sam has no modern conveniences, he has little time to relax or enjoy his environment. Take a few minutes to briefly outline in the left column below a typical day for Sam.   Be sure to include all the important tasks that Sam routinely has to complete. After you have completed the outline, in the right column explain how each of Sam's activities would be accomplished in your house. Beside each task, estimate how long it would take you to do these activities.

Sam's Typical Day	At My House	Time

Assuming that all of the tasks are completed within the fourteen hours of daylight, how much time would you have left over for relaxing? _____

Name_____

Animal vs. Human Behavior

In his writings, Sam makes some interesting observations about human and animal behaviors. Read the quotes written below. Use examples from the text and your own experiences to explain what Sam means.

1. "I can only say that after living so long with the birds and animals, the movement of a human is like the difference between the explosion of a cap pistol and a cannon." (Chapter 8)

   _____

   _____

   _____

   _____

   _____

2. "There is something human about his beady glance. Perhaps because that glance tells me something. It tells me he knows who I am and that he does not want me to come any closer." (Chapter 14)

   _____

   _____

   _____

   _____

   _____

3. "The chickadees, like the people on Third Avenue, had their favorite routes to and from the best food supplies." (Chapter 18)

   _____

   _____

   _____

   _____

   _____

Look through the novel to find other quotes describing human and animal behaviors that interest you. Discuss these quotes with a partner.

Name_____

Independence

In the final chapter of *My Side of the Mountain*, Sam's family arrives and begins to set up housekeeping in the Catskills. Sam's father brings a pack full of food as well as lumber to build a house. Sam's mother went so far as to say, "Well, if he doesn't want to come home, then we will bring home to him." Sam is stunned by his family's plan. For the past year he has thrived on his independence and has survived under difficult conditions by himself. What do you think will happen to Sam's independence now that his family is sharing his home?

Write some of your ideas in the space provided below.

_____
_____
_____
_____
_____
_____
_____
_____
_____
_____
_____
_____
_____
_____
_____
_____
_____
_____

Now, pair up with a partner to discuss your ideas and write the next chapter of *My Side of the Mountain*.

Lost on a Mountain in Maine

by Donn Fendler and Joseph B. Egan

(Beech Tree, 1992)

(Available in Canada: Gage Distributors; the United Kingdom: International Book Distributors; Australia: Kirby Book Co.)

Lost on a Mountain in Maine is the true story of how a 12 year old boy survived alone in the wilderness of Maine for nine days. Donn Fendler left his hiking group and became lost in the fog, sleet, and rain on top of Baxter State Park's Mt. Katahdin. He wandered aimlessly while looking for a trail, and finally he left the mountain plateau and went in the deep woods. Once below the tree line, he wandered where no trails existed, following streams and blown down phone wires. He ate wild berries and drank stream water. Wearing only a light windbreaker, he had little protection from the environment. His hope of finding civilization around each bend in the stream kept him moving. After nine days of wandering, Donn stumbled to the edge of the Penobscot River where Mr. McMoarn found him and took him to his cabin for medical attention.

Name_____

Donn's Trail Map

We use maps as a way of recording the land around us. They can be used as directional guides or as a source for monitoring changes in our surroundings. Every map has a key or legend. The key contains important information about how to read the map. Most keys have a listing of the symbols on the map and their meanings, a distance scale, and a compass rose. Maps are sometimes divided into quadrants to aid the reader in finding a location quickly. The quadrant is found by following the lettered and numbered lines at the edges of the map. A quadrant is defined by listing both the letter and the number that correspond to the area.

Maine guides and rangers traced Donn's approximate trek through Baxter State Park. They sketched this map of his journey. Use the information in this map to answer the questions below.

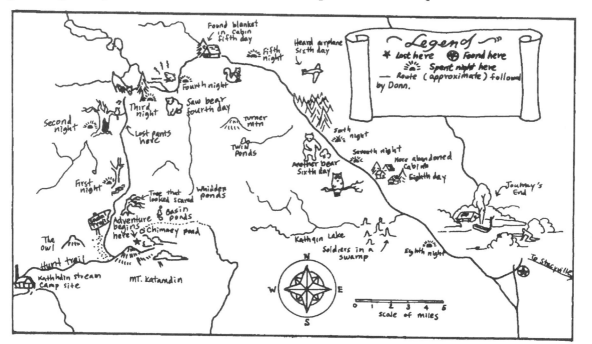

1. About how many miles/kilometers does Donn travel in the first day? _____

2. How many times does he see bears? _____

3. What is the name of the stream that he follows for most of his trek? _____

4. In what quadrant does Donn spend his third night? _____

5. What direction would you travel to reach Bangor from Mt. Katahdin? _____

6. Name one landmark that is located in quadrant B,4. _____

7. What symbol does the map use to represent where Donn sleeps? _____

Challenge: Work in teams to draw your own map of a location in your neighborhood. Be sure to locate the direction of north first so your map will be positioned correctly.

Name_____

Journal

When Donn became separated from his hiking party, he made many mistakes that almost cost him his life. Many of these mistakes were made because of Donn's inexperience with wilderness survival and his unfamiliarity with the region in which he was lost. Donn was lucky to have survived. How would you have coped in Donn's situation? What might you have done differently?

Use the journal writing space below to outline the events that Donn experienced. Make stars next to the events that you feel occurred as a result of Donn's poor judgment. Explain what you might have done instead if you had been in his place.

Name_____

Balanced Diet

The food pyramid is based on a healthy, well-balanced diet. It is important to eat a balanced diet of foods to remain healthy and strong. Some food groups are more important to our diets than others, so we should try to eat more foods from these groups. Other food groups are less important, and these foods should be eaten sparingly.

Food Pyramid

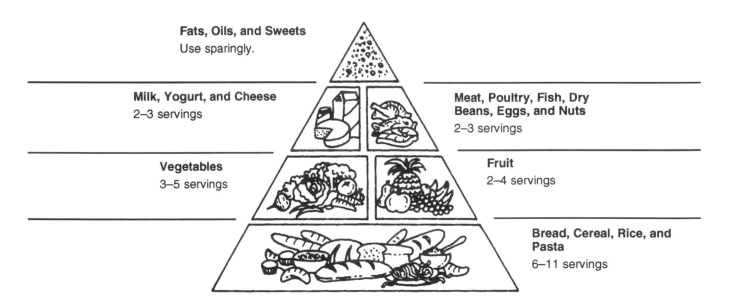

Fats, Oils, and Sweets
Use sparingly.

Milk, Yogurt, and Cheese
2–3 servings

Meat, Poultry, Fish, Dry Beans, Eggs, and Nuts
2–3 servings

Vegetables
3–5 servings

Fruit
2–4 servings

Bread, Cereal, Rice, and Pasta
6–11 servings

1. Donn scavenges for his food while he is lost in the Maine woods. Make a list of the foods that Donn eats during the nine days he is lost.

    _____

    _____

    _____

    _____

    _____

2. Is Donn's diet healthy? _____

3. What food groups does Donn's diet lack? _____

    _____

    _____

4. Choose one day and list all of the foods that you eat during that day. Use the chart on the next page. In the snack category, list any foods eaten outside of the three regular mealtimes.

Balanced Diet *(cont.)*

	Your Menu
Breakfast	
Lunch	
Dinner	
Snacks	

5. Do you eat a well-balanced diet? _____

6. a. If not, what food groups do you need to eat more of? _____

    _____

    _____

    b. What food groups do you need to eat less of? _____

    _____

    _____

Name_____

Lost

There are few situations more frightening than being lost. When Donn was lost for nine days, he did not know where he was nor did his family know where to find him. Many of the people searching for Donn thought that he must be dead.

Remember a time when you or someone you loved was lost. How did you feel? What did you think? What did you do?

The following is a list of common rules to remember if you become lost in the wilderness and you know that someone will soon miss you. Note the rules which Donn did not follow and discuss what he did instead.

1. If you become separated from your group, stay put. Your group will have a better chance of finding you if you do not move.

2. Stay on the marked trail if you are on one.

3. Stay calm and do not panic.

4. Use the universal distress code. This is a signal repeated three times. You can either yell, use a whistle, or set out a marking on open ground.

5. Keep warm, dry, and comfortable.

Although we never plan to become lost, it is always good to be prepared for emergencies when we are hiking. Make a list of five preparations that Donn could have made before becoming lost that might have helped him enhance his chances for survival.

a. _____

_____

b. _____

_____

c. _____

_____

d. _____

_____

e. _____

_____

Name_____

Scouting

The first scouting organization was established by Robert Baden-Powell in Great Britain in 1907. After returning from a tour of duty as a soldier in India, he decided that he would like to help the British youth become better citizens. He invited 22 boys to spend a week on an island off the coast of England with the goal of teaching woodcraft, lifesaving, and nature observation. Following this camp, he wrote the book *Scouting for Boys*. Boys all over England read the book and became excited about scouting. Boy Scout troops were soon organized all over the country.

While on a trip, American businessman William D. Boyce met one of Mr. Baden-Powell's British scouts. Mr. Boyce was lost in the streets of London and asked the boy for directions. He was so impressed with the boy's helpfulness that he asked to meet with the scout leader, Mr. Baden-Powell. After learning more about the scouting organization, Mr. Boyce returned to America and founded the Boy Scouts of America on February 8, 1910. The primary goal of this organization was to develop the "character, citizenship, and physical fitness of America's youth."

Since 1910, scouting has grown. Summer camps have been established, troops have been designed for boys younger than eleven, and the Girl Scouts of America was founded in 1912. Today, millions of youth worldwide participate in scouting organizations.

The following is a copy of the Boy Scout Oath. Read the oath and then think about how it and the organization the oath represents might have helped Donn survive while he was lost in the woods. Write your ideas below. Then, research to find out more about the scouting organizations in your area and what they are doing to help your community.

> *On my honor, I will do my best*
> *To do my duty to God and my country*
> *and to obey the Scout law;*
> *To help other people at all times;*
> *To keep myself physically strong,*
> *mentally awake, and morally straight.*

_____

_____

_____

_____

_____

_____

_____

_____

Name_____

Dated Language

Lost on a Mountain in Maine was first written and published in 1939. Although this story occurred many years ago, it is still being published, read, and marveled at by people today. Can you think of any other stories that have lasted over the years? Why do you think they have? Discuss this with the class.

Since *Lost on a Mountain in Maine* was written so long ago, the text includes many slang expressions, descriptions or phrases that are not common in our language today. Read the sentences from the story listed below. Each contains a word or phrase that may sound unusual to you. Rewrite the sentences so they sound more like something someone might say today. Look through the text to see if you find any other unusual words that would be uncommon in our language today.

1. "It kind of scares a fellow, especially when you are alone and awfully cold."

   _____

2. "The sleet formed slick, thin ice on the sleeves of my reefer, and I had to wipe it off my face."

   _____

3. "Dungarees are all right for dry hikes, but they're terrible when they get cold and wet."

   _____

4. "Christmas! I was surprised. Those sneakers were slashed all over."

   _____

5. "You see, at that time I didn't really think I was in a bad fix."

   _____

6. "Funny how you can get chummy with the wild animals when you're in the woods."

   _____

7. "The next thing I really remember was Mrs. McMoarn. She was grand."

   _____

8. "I heard the telephone ringing like mad..."

   _____

Name_____

Who is Donn?

Read and respond to the following questions about Donn Fendler. Be sure to use examples from the text to support your answers. When you are finished, share your answers with the class.

1. Donn Fendler survived for nine days with almost no food and no shelter. Even his clothing was in rags and provided very little protection from the environment. What kept Donn from giving up and just lying down in the woods to die? _____

   _____

   _____

   _____

2. List five values that were important to Donn. Explain why they were important. _____

   _____

   _____

   _____

3. Drawing upon the text, give a physical description of Donn Fendler. _____

   _____

   _____

   _____

4. If you could have met Donn Fendler when he was twelve years old, do you think you would have been friends? Explain. _____

   _____

   _____

   _____

5. Why did Donn's story attract so much attention from the media? Can you think of any current survival story that has attracted media attentions? _____

   _____

   _____

   _____

Name _____

Insects

Insects are found everywhere in the world. Through research, entomologists have discovered and described over 600,000 kinds of insects. No matter where you go, there are insects sharing your environment. In *Lost on a Mountain in Maine*, Donn describes his miserable experiences with the insect pests commonly found in the woods of New England. He is bitten and stung until his skin is red and swollen. Although Donn is annoyed and irritated by the mosquitoes, blackflies, and moose flies in the woods, the insects do not have a deadly effect. Although the insects are not deadly, they do have an impact on Donn. How do the insects affect Donn's ultimate quest for survival?

_____
_____
_____
_____
_____
_____
_____
_____
_____

We all are annoyed by insects that pester us in our own communities. What insect pests live in your region? How do you cope with them? Could you tolerate these insects for nine straight days with no relief?

_____
_____
_____
_____
_____
_____
_____
_____

Name_____

Senses

When people become frightened, their senses become enhanced. People can often see, hear, and smell things that they might not notice if they were not frightened. This is because of a natural physical change that occurs in the body as a self-defense mechanism. Fright causes stress to the body, and as a result of stress, the body releases adrenaline or epinephrine from the adrenal gland. This chemical has several effects on the body. It prepares the body for defense by stimulating the heart, constricting blood vessels, raising blood pressure, and releasing sugars into the blood stream. These physical changes help prepare the body by making it more alert and, thus, better able to cope with uncertain situations. You may remember a time when you were in a frightening situation and you could hear your own heart beating. Your breathing became shallower, and you had a strong awareness of everything around you. The release of adrenaline is one of the ways your body naturally prepares for survival.

Although Donn dictates his story to Joseph Egan weeks after the event, he still recalls several vivid images. In many of Donn's descriptions, he emphasizes how he feels, what he sees, what he hears, or what he smells. As you read these examples from the text, think about how Donn must feel and what he is thinking about his own survival.

- "I listened. Only the whining noise of the wind in the stunted trees—no, there was another noise—rocks falling, far off to the right—a slow, heavy crunching sound—then silence, deeper than before."

- "The wind was sharp, and it blew so hard that the rain and sleet stung like needles."

- "I never smelled anything so bad as that blanket. I almost had to hold my nose, but I went to sleep just the same."

- "I climbed onto a tree trunk and I could see a big bog full of dead trees. Each one looked like a soldier. The sun was shining on them and some of the branches looked like silver."

Now, think of a time when you were very frightened. Close your eyes. What images, sounds, smells, and tastes do you recall? Do a free write below and on the back of this page. When you are finished, underline all the words which represent the awareness of your five senses.

_____

_____

_____

_____

_____

_____

Arctic Survival

Name_____

The Arctic

The Arctic is technically defined as being the area around the North Pole to approximately 65°N latitude. This is the point at which the Arctic Circle encircles the earth. The Arctic Circle passes through the United States, Canada, Greenland, Sweden, Finland, Norway, and Russia.

What are the people like who live in this region of the world? What do they eat? What are their homes like? What do they do for jobs and entertainment? How do they survive the sub-zero temperatures of winter?

Use the information you already know and logic to fill in the chart below in response to these questions. Then, search in resource books to confirm, modify, or disprove your responses.

	What I know	What I think I know	What I want to know
People			
Food			
Homes			
Jobs/ Entertainment			
Winter Survival			

Name _____

Winter and Summer Solstices

The summer solstice occurs when the sun is at the northernmost point on its *ecliptic*, its pathway across the horizon. This happens on June 21. On this day, there are 24 hours of daylight at points above the Arctic Circle. The weeks leading up to this date are marked by gradually extending hours of daylight. The winter solstice occurs when the sun is at the southernmost point on its ecliptic. This happens on December 21 and results in 24 hours of darkness in the Arctic. The weeks leading to this date are marked by gradually shortening hours of daylight.

Imagine that you are living in the Arctic Circle. What would it be like adjusting to 24 hours of sunlight? What would it be like living in constant darkness? Make a list of the activities that would be difficult to do under the extremes of each of these conditions and how you might accommodate for these difficulties.

24 Hours Daylight	24 Hours Darkness

Use these lists to write two paragraphs. In one, describe how you might pass a day in the Arctic on June 22. In the second, describe your day on December 22.

Name_____

Frostbite

If you have spent time outside on extremely cold days, you may have had some experience with frostbite. Frostbite is the most common injury resulting from overexposure to the cold. It is caused by the freezing of fluids in the skin tissue. As frostbite is setting in, the skin usually turns a flushed color. The exposed area then turns a grayish yellow and begins to feel cold and numb. Sometimes the area becomes slightly painful. If left untreated, blisters will form on the skin, and blood will not be able to circulate to the region. In extreme cases, there is permanent damage to the skin tissue, and the exposed area may have to be removed.

First aid for frostbite is fairly simple. First, cover the frostbitten area. Warm the victim by wrapping him or her in a blanket or coat and taking him or her inside a shelter. You might want to give the person something hot to drink. Begin to rewarm the frostbitten area by submerging it in warm (not hot) water. Be careful not to expose the frostbitten area to extreme heat. This can damage the skin. Do not rub the frozen area. This can also damage the skin. Continue rewarming the area until it has returned to its normal color. If the frostbite damage is severe or extensive, professional medical help may be necessary.

If you were planning a trip to the Arctic, what precautions might you take to protect yourself from frostbite?

_____

_____

_____

_____

What extra first aid items might you want to consider taking along to prevent and treat frostbite? Explain the purpose of each of these items.

Item   **Purpose**

_____   _____

_____   _____

_____   _____

_____   _____

_____   _____

_____   _____

_____   _____

Make a Compass

The compass was invented by the Chinese over 1,000 years ago. A magician made the discovery that when a game piece was set on a table, it would always turn to face north. The Chinese thought this was magic. Actually, the game piece was made of lodestone. Lodestone is a natural iron ore which is magnetic.

Every magnet has two poles. One pole is positive, and one is negative. The earth also has two poles which are magnetic. These are the North and the South Poles. A magnetic compass needle is drawn to the North Pole and will always point north. Once a person knows which direction is north, he or she can find the south, east, and west.

You can make your own magnetic compass by following these directions.

Materials: a clear bowl, a magnet, a needle, water, paper, a cork, and a pencil

Directions:

1. Fill the bowl with water and place it on the blank piece of paper.

2. Rub one end of the magnet along the needle. Be sure to rub the magnet in the same direction each time. Do this about 30 times.

3. Stick the needle through the center of the cork.

4. Place the cork in the water bowl.

5. Watch to see which way the needle points. Use a standard compass to check which end of the needle is pointing north.

6. Write *N, S, E,* and *W* on the piece of paper beneath the bowl to correspond with the direction of the needle.

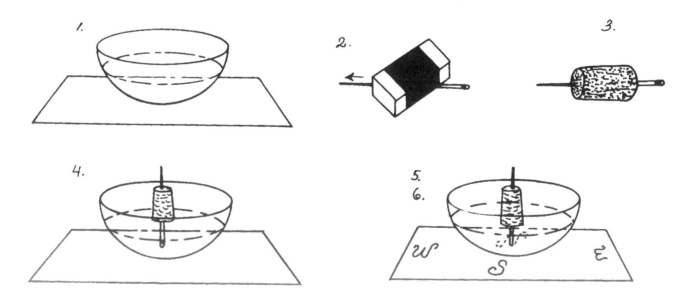

Name_____

Using Your Compass

A compass needle will always point to magnetic north. To use your compass (page 66), face the landmark that you wish to locate. Hold the compass flat in your hand. Slowly turn the compass until the needle points to the letter N. Make an imaginary line on the compass face from the center to the outer edge in the direction of your landmark. Read the letters on the compass nearest to the line. (If you have a compass with a line marking the direction of travel, line this up with the landmark before you begin. You can use this to read your direction more accurately.)

There are eight main directional points on a compass: north, south, east, west, northeast, northwest, southeast, and southwest. The face of the compass is also divided into 360 degrees, or points. These degrees are used to find the "bearing" of a distant object. The bearing tells you how far an object is from magnetic north.

Practice using your compass by doing the following activity. Stand in the center of your classroom. Record the directions of the objects listed below. If you have a compass that marks degrees, also note the bearings of the objects. Add three objects of your choice to the list.

1. chalkboard   _____

2. waste basket   _____

3. teacher's desk   _____

4. front door   _____

5. windows   _____

6. _____   _____

7. _____   _____

8. _____   _____

When you have mastered the use of your compass in the classroom, identify three landmarks that you can see from your school yard. Stand in the center of the yard and record the direction of each of these objects.

1. _____   _____

2. _____   _____

3. _____   _____

Topographic Maps

A topographic map is used to record the elevations of a region. By reading the lines and colors on a map, a person is able to determine where mountains, canyons, and plains exist. On a tundra wasteland or in the mountains where snow makes it difficult to locate landmarks, a topographical map showing the elevations of the area can be a helpful tool. Try this activity to understand how the lines on a topographic map define elevation.

You will need a washable marker and your hand. Make a fist with your knuckles facing up. Take your marker and draw a small circle on your highest knuckle. Draw another circle around this circle. Be sure to keep the lines level. When you begin to trace your third or fourth circle, you may need to go around more than one knuckle to keep your marks level. You will also find that you will need to draw your lines inward when you come to the valleys between your fingers. Continue drawing circles until you have included all of your knuckles. Now lay your hand flat and look at the lines. The lines represent the mountains and valleys of your fist.

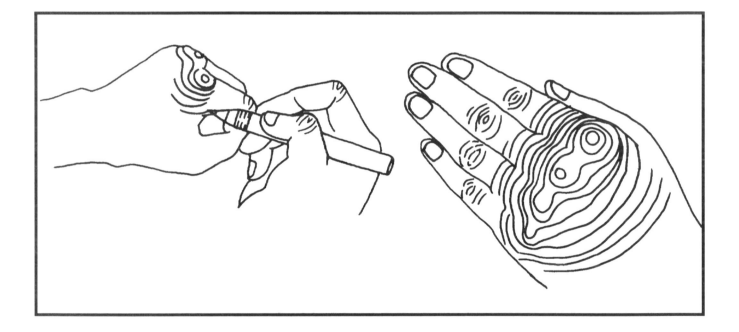

Study some actual topographical maps. Then draw a topographical map showing the elevation changes in your neighborhood. (You might want to start with a local map that marks the streets. Then sketch in the lines representing elevation highs and lows.)

Name_____

Clothing

While it is less important in southern regions, in the Arctic, proper clothing is necessary for survival. The Inuit tribe which inhabits the Arctic region from Alaska to Siberia has a standard costume for the harsh environment. They wear watertight boots, double-layered trousers, and a hooded parka consisting of double layers of furs and skin. Both men and women wear these clothes. What benefits do you think this combination of clothing provides for the Inuit people in the Arctic? Discuss this with the class.

Think about clothing materials with which you are familiar. Which of these materials or combination of materials would provide the most protection in a cold climate? Circle the most protective and then explain your choices.

- wool
- cotton
- silk
- Gor-tex®
- polyester
- fur
- nylon
- leather
- rayon
- flannel
- rubber
- linen

What would you wear if you were planning a trip to the Arctic?

_____

_____

_____

_____

_____

_____

Why would you select these clothes?

_____

_____

_____

_____

_____

_____

_____

Name_____

Robert E. Peary and Matthew Henson

Robert E. Peary made six attempts to reach the North Pole between the years of 1891 and 1909. His companion and close assistant on each of these trips was a young man named Matthew Henson. On his sixth attempt, Peary finally had success. In February of 1909, Peary left Cape Columbia with a group of Inuit tribesmen and his assistants. They carried supplies and traveled by sledges pulled by dogs. After battling the sub-zero temperatures, conquering the massive ice drifts, and losing one of the group in an accident, Peary's expedition arrived at the North Pole on April 6, 1909. This was the first recognized group of men to stand on the polar icecap.

Research to find out more about these arctic explorers and the hardships they endured. Would you have been interested in joining one of Peary's exploration parties? Why or why not?

Name_____

Temperature Conversions

In arctic regions, the temperature in the wintertime seldom rises above 32°F or 0°C. It is almost always below freezing. To live in these regions takes a hardy individual.

In order to understand a little more about temperature, do the exercises below. The equations you will need are in the following boxes.

To convert Celsius to Fahrenheit:

Multiply the temperature times $^9/_5$ and add 32.

($^9/_5$ x temperature) + 32 = Fahrenheit

To calculate Fahrenheit to Celsius:

Subtract 32 from the temperature and then multiply by $^9/_5$.

(temperature – 32) x $^9/_5$ = Celsius

A. Convert the following temperatures from Celsius to Fahrenheit.

1. The coldest temperature ever recorded in the arctic region was in Northeastern Siberia. It was – 68°C. _____

2. The coldest temperature ever recorded in the North American Arctic region was in the Yukon Territory. It was – 65°C. _____

B. Convert the average winter temperature ranges for these towns in Alaska from Fahrenheit to Celsius.

1. Naknek: 14°F to 24°F   _____

2. Fairbanks: –17°F to 8°F   _____

3. Noatak: –20°F to –2°F   _____

4. Anchorage: 4°F to 26°F   _____

5. Juneau: 20°F to 32°F   _____

Name_____

True North

Although a compass needle will be drawn to magnetic north and will point to the correct general direction, topographic maps are more precisely oriented to true north. True north is the exact point where the North Pole is located. The earth's natural magnetic pull is actually over 1,000 miles (1,600 km) southwest of the North Pole. Depending upon where you are standing in the United States, your compass needle will vary anywhere from 20°W to 20°E of true north. We call the angle between true north and magnetic north the *declination*. The declination is measured in degrees.

You can adjust for the difference between true north and magnetic north by calculating the declination. A topographic map will usually note the declination of the region in the legend. The map below shows the declinations for the United States. Use the information on the map to answer the questions.

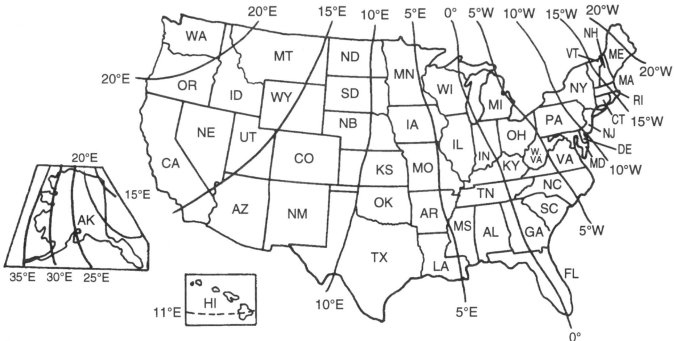

Answer:

1. In which state(s) is there the greatest degree of declination? How much? Draw the angles that represent the difference.

_____

2. In which state(s) is there the least degree of declination? How much?

_____

3. Approximately what degree of declination is your town? How much? Draw the angle that represents the difference.

_____

Challenge: Bring in a topographic map of your region. Note the declination. Use a compass to take a bearing and accurately calculate the difference between true north and magnetic north.

Three-Dimensional Map

Sometimes we use maps that show land contours with actual elevation. You can make your own three-dimensional topographic map using the recipe and directions below.

Materials:

- piece of heavy cardboard
- paint
- stove / hot plate
- pot for mixing dough
- food coloring

Play Dough Ingredients:

- 1 cup (250 mL) flour
- ½ cup (125 mL) salt
- 1 tbls. (15 mL) cooking oil
- 1 tbls. (15 mL) cream of tartar
- 1 cup (250 mL) water

Directions:

Mix dry ingredients with the oil. Add the water. Cook over medium heat, stirring constantly until dough is stiff. Take dough out of the pot and knead it until it is has the consistency of a play dough. (If you want to add food coloring instead of painting the final product, you can color your dough as it is cooking.)

Spread the dough on the cardboard to form your map. You can shape mountains and valleys on the flat surface by molding the dough. You can also add trees, rocks, or other landmarks while the dough is still soft. When it is dry, you can paint the surface to look like your landscape.

(The dough can be made in advance and packaged in airtight plastic bags for later use.)

Igloos

Although Inuit tribe members of Eastern and Central Canada now live in modern homes, there was a time when they built and lived in houses made out of objects in their environment. In the summer, they built houses of sod and skins. In the winter, they built houses of rock, snow, and wood. On long winter journeys, they built temporary or emergency dome-shaped shelters of snow. The Inuit call these shelters *iglu*, which means *house*. An igloo can be built anywhere there is snow and provide the shelter necessary for survival.

Igloos are made by cutting blocks of deep, hard-packed snow. The blocks are then placed in a circle to form a base. A doorway is left on the side away from the wind. (Usually a tunnel of blocks is made to protect this entrance from the wind.) Layers of blocks are placed on the foundation. Each layer is laid in tightly by packing snow into the crevices. As the dome is formed, each layer is molded to pitch in slightly until the circle of blocks meets at the top of the dome. An air hole is made in the roof for ventilation.

If you live in an area where there is snow, you can try to build your own igloo. If you do not have snow available, try to build a model of an igloo by using sugar cubes. Use glue to hold each layer in place.

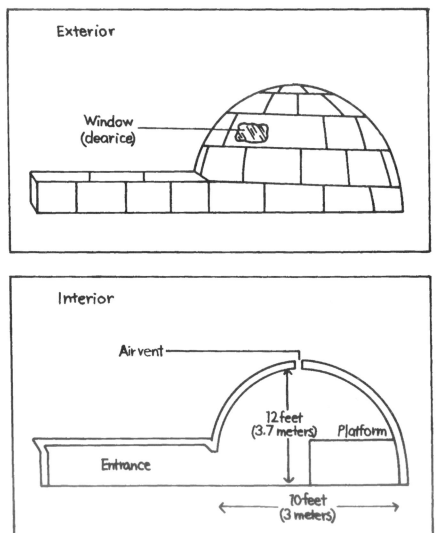

Name_____

Heart Rate

When you are in a cold climate, it is easy for your body to become cold if you sit still too long. By moving, you increase your heart rate. As your heart rate increases, your heart pumps more blood faster, and your body becomes warmer. If you have proper clothing, you can keep yourself warm just by exercising. Although it is good to keep your body warm in sub-zero temperatures, you can defeat the purpose if your body creates too much sweat. The sweat can begin to freeze on your skin and chill your body.

Do the following exercises in sequence. Take your pulse after each and record the number of beats per minute in the first column. (You can save time by taking your pulse for 15 seconds and multiplying the total by 4.) In the second column, write a brief statement regarding how warm you feel and how much you are sweating.

Activity	Heart Rate	Comments
1. resting pulse (sitting quietly)		
2. walking for 5 minutes		
3. doing 10 sit-ups and 10 push-ups		
4. walking up and down the stairs for 5 minutes		
5. jumping rope for 5 minutes		
6. running for 10 minutes		

When you have completed your chart, look at the relationship between your heart rate and the comments you made. Does the relationship tell you anything?

Julie of the Wolves

by Jean Craighead George

(Harper and Row, 1972)

(Available in Canada and Australia: HarperCollins; the United Kingdom: Cornerstone Books)

As a child, Miyax enjoys living with her father, Kapugen, in the fishing village. Surrounded by her elders, Miyax learns about the traditional ways. Her father teaches her to fish, dance, sing, and sew. But most importantly, Kapugen teaches Miyax to watch and learn from the animals. When Miyax turns nine, her aunt arrives in the fishing camp saying that Miyax must attend school. Miyax is sent to live with her aunt. Now that Miyax is living in a large village and is learning English, her family and friends call her Julie instead of her Eskimo name. In school, Julie learns about the Western culture and the modern ways of living. She corresponds with a pen pal in San Francisco and thinks it would be nice to live with this pen pal in her beautiful modern home. However, when Julie turns thirteen, she is sent to live with one of Kapugen's friends and is married to his son. Julie is unhappy and decides to run away to San Francisco. She packs a minimal survival pack and leaves in the night. But soon after she loses sight of the village, she finds that she is lost in the Alaskan wilderness with no food, water, or compass. Fortunately, Miyax comes upon a pack of wolves. She spends days observing the wolves, and through patience and practice, she learns to communicate with them. The wolves accept Julie as one of them and allow her to share their food. Julie survives day to day by testing her own survival instincts and by applying what she has learned from her father. Through her experience, she gains a renewed respect for the traditional ways of her people. She learns about the basic necessities of survival and enjoys the beauty of her culture.

Alaska Map

When Miyax runs away, she is in the northernmost region of Alaska. Locate her approximate location on this map. Then, research to find out more about this wilderness area. Also research to find out how long it would take Miyax to travel by ship from Alaska to San Francisco.

Name_____

Compact Bodies

Miyax is described as having a body which is slightly short-limbed and compact. As with many of the Arctic region creatures, Miyax's body is built to conserve heat. Heat conservation is necessary for survival in the Arctic. If the body core, or center, becomes too cold, the body will fall into shock and die. The body attempts to regulate temperature by dispersing heat from the body core. By having a body with short arms and legs, the body has less surface area over which to spread its heat.

Research the list of animals below. Identify those that are native to the Arctic region. How are their bodies shaped? Are they built to conserve heat, or do they have other ways to keep warm in the frigid Arctic climate?

	Native: yes or no	Body Shape	Conserve Heat: yes or no
1. polar bear			
2. bobcat			
3. penguin			
4. iguana			
5. skunk			
6. rattlesnake			
7. lemming			
8. Siberian tiger			
9. rabbit			
10. bat			
11. muskrat			
12. adder snake			
13. seal			
14. walrus			
15. weasel			
16. wolverine			
17. sloth			
18. reindeer			
19. caribou			
20. moose			
21. elk			
22. beaver			
23. coyote			

Name_____

Symbolism

A symbol is a person, situation, idea, or place that implies more than one meaning within the context of a story. The symbol has a literal, or real, meaning and a figurative, or deeper, meaning. For example, a dove is a bird, but we also recognize the dove as being a symbol for peace. Writers integrate symbols into their stories to enrich the meaning of their text. The overtones of familiar symbols in a piece of writing contribute to the fluency and understanding of the reader.

As you read *Julie of the Wolves*, look for these symbols. Explain both their literal and figurative meanings. Space is left for you to add any additional symbols that you may discover while reading.

	Literal Meaning	Figurative Meaning
1. San Francisco		
2. Jello		
3. seal camp		
4. lemmings		
5. airplane		
6. oil drum		
7. Tornait		

Pen Pals

As Miyax returns home from her job at the hospital one day, a man hands her a letter. He tells her that the girl who wrote the letter would like to become pen pals with a girl her own age in Alaska. Miyax writes to her new friend and learns about life in San Francisco.

Pen pals are a great way for students to learn about different people, cultures, and areas of the country. Contact one of the agencies listed below to match your class with another. You may wish to request a certain region which will tie in with a future social studies unit.

Note: To ensure that the agency you write to is still in operation, please contact it before beginning this activity with your class.

International Friendship League

55 Mount Vernon Street
Boston, MA 02108

This organization pairs American students with pen pals in 127 different countries. Margaret MacDonough is the executive director.

World Pen Pals

1690 Como Avenue
Saint Paul, MN 55108
(612) 647–0191

This organization pairs students ages 12–20 worldwide. A processing fee of $2.50 per student is required, or $3.00 per student if there are fewer than six in the class.

FrEdMail

FrEdMail is an exciting way to integrate your correspondences with computer technology. FrEdMail stands for Free Educational Electronic Mail and is a free service offered to educators. Using this system, students can communicate around the world through computer electronic bulletin boards. FrEdMail has bulletin boards in about 30 states with over 300 sites worldwide, and offers many opportunities for shared study projects. To find out more about FrEdMail, call 619-475-4852. This is a Southern California location.

Name_____

Body Language

Miyax learns to communicate with the wolves by using body language. Through observation, she learns that certain body movements have meanings to the wolves.

We all use body language in our daily lives as a way to communicate with one another more effectively. Without the use of movements, sometimes our words might be confused or misinterpreted. What are some of the meanings for the body language listed below? (Some of the motions may have several meanings and would require more explanation, such as a word or additional motion, for another person to fully understand the "speaker.")

Motion	Meanings
1. nodding head	
2. shaking head	
3. shrugging shoulders	
4. thumb up	
5. thumb down	
6. crossed arms	
7. crossed fingers	
8. slouching in chair	
9. hands on hips	
10. smiling	
11. bunched up eyebrows	
12. arms outstretched	
13. pointing finger	
14. hands behind back	
15. clapping hands	
16. bowing head	
17. stomping foot	
18. clenching fist	

Name_____

Relationships

When Miyax discusses her relationship with Kapu, she tells him about an Eskimo saying. She says, "We Eskimos have joking partners—people to have fun with—and serious partners—people to work and think with." She tells Kapu that he is the best kind of partner because she likes to both joke and be serious with him. We all know people with whom we can work and people with whom we can joke. Sometimes it is difficult to mix working and joking with these people.

Think of your friends. Are there some friends with whom you would go to the movies but would have a difficult time working with on a project at school? What do you think about when you choose a partner for a project? When you work with a joking friend, is your school work as successful?

Think about these questions, then make lists of the traits of a working friend and of a joking friend.

Working Friend	Joking Friend

Do you have any friends who have traits from both of these categories?

Name_____

Traditions

Traditions are patterns of behaviors, beliefs, or actions that have been passed down from one generation to the next within a certain cultural group. It is the traditions within a culture that identify and bond a group of people.

As a young child, Miyax learns about the traditions of her culture. She learns to dance, sing, and make an *i'noGo tied*. Miyax is a member of her group. During her adolescence, Miyax is separated from her group and placed with people who do not understand her traditions. Among her new peers, she is embarrassed by her old traditions because they seem simple. As a response to her frustration, she throws away her *i'noGo tied*. It is not until years later that she learns to appreciate and embrace the richness of her Eskimo heritage.

Every family or group has traditions which are important. What traditions do you value? How does following these traditions help you identify as a member of your group? Write your traditions here. Then, share some of these traditions with your classmates.

_____

_____

_____

_____

_____

_____

_____

_____

_____

_____

_____

_____

_____

_____

Read back through *Julie of the Wolves* and make a list on the back of this paper of all the traditions that Miyax adopts from her Eskimo heritage.

Name _____

Survival Tools

When Jello steals Miyax's pack, she is frantic. She knows that she cannot replace the items in her pack, and without these items it will be extremely difficult for her to survive. Although the items in her pack are simple tools, they are the basic tools for survival.

Identify the tools listed below and explain the value of each item.

1. needles _____

_____

2. boots_____

_____

3. ulo _____

_____

4. matches _____

_____

Describe modern tools that you might carry in place of these Eskimo tools.

_____

_____

_____

_____

_____

_____

_____

_____

_____

_____

Storytelling Dance

After Kapu brings Miyax the leg of a caribou, Miyax is inspired to dance. She performs a series of steps that she remembers learning when she was a young girl in the seal camp. As part of her dance, she improvises and tells the story of how a wolf brought meat to a young girl.

For centuries, dancing has been a rich part of many cultures. It has been performed in religious ceremonies to appease and thank the gods, in celebrations to tell stories, and in daily life to communicate ideas. Read about the following people and some of the reasons for their dances.

- The Hopi tribes of northeastern Arizona perform a *snake dance*. This dance is performed every two years as a request to the gods for rain. In this dance, the participants handle live snakes. The snakes represent the children of their ancestors who were turned into snakes and therefore have magical powers.

- In Bali, the people perform a dance called the *barong*. The goal of this dance is to drive evil spirits from the village.

- Hawaiians dance the *hula* as a way of storytelling. This dance involves a combination of gestures and chanting. By combining six basic movements in several different ways, the dancers tell of the mythological stories of their culture.

- In Africa, the Chi Wara dance on their agricultural fields. This is in honor of the man who created agriculture and is also a reminder to the farmers about how difficult it is to work the fields each year.

Create and design your own story dance. You can use one of the fairy tale ideas listed below or come up with one of your own. When you have designed your dance, share it with your class. Have them try to tell your story as you dance.

- *The Three Pigs*
- *Little Red Riding Hood*
- *Jack and the Beanstalk*
- *Cinderella*
- *Sleeping Beauty*
- *Seven in One Blow*
- *Rumplestilskin*
- *Goldilocks and the Three Bears*
- *Princess and the Pea*
- *Little Red Hen*
- *Chicken Little*

Name_____

Closure

After Tornait dies, Miyax sings a song to Amoraq. Although she has been speaking in Upick, her native language, for the past several months, she chooses to sing this final song in English. Also, in the last sentence she is referred to as Julie instead of Miyax. Turn to the last page of *Julie of the Wolves* and respond to Miyax's final song in freewrite form. Save this freewrite for class discussion.

_____

_____

_____

_____

_____

_____

_____

_____

_____

_____

_____

_____

_____

_____

_____

_____

_____

_____

_____

_____

Maroo of the Winter Caves

by Ann Turnbull

(Clarion Books, 1984)

(Available in Canada: Thomas Allen & Son; the United Kingdom: Gollancz Services; Australia: Jackaranda Wiley)

The setting of *Maroo of the Winter Caves* is Europe at the end of the last ice age. Snow and glaciers still cover much of the European landscape during the long winter months. Maroo is a member of one of the nomadic tribes which wander throughout the region. During the winter, Maroo and her family share a home in the caves above the frozen wasteland. The men from many families hunt together, and the women work to prepare food for the group. Everyone depends upon one another. During the summer months, all of the families depart from the protection of the winter caves to forage for food and to enjoy the changes that summer brings to the land below. Although Maroo's mother is expecting a baby, Maroo's family decides to travel to the ocean. Late in the summer, a baby boy is born. Unfortunately, the late birth of the child has delayed the family's return to the winter caves. They leave the ocean, traveling as quickly as they are able with a newborn child. On the return trip, Maroo's father is killed, and her brother is injured while hunting. A few days later, the family is caught in a blizzard, still days away from the other members of their tribe. They are out of food and have no way to hunt. Old Mother decides that Maroo and her brother must be sent for help if the family has any hopes for survival. They build a snow house, and Maroo and Otak set off with their dog, Rivo, to travel over the mountain alone. The two children suffer hunger and perils in their travels. Maroo is almost suffocated when she falls into a glacial crevice, and they are trapped for two days on the mountaintop by a raging blizzard. On the fourth day out, Otak and Rivo become lost, and Maroo must go on without her brother to find help. She arrives safely in the village and guides members of the tribe back to help her family. As the village feasts and mourns the death of Maroo's brother, Otak walks into the circle and tells how Rivo saved his life by hunting for food and keeping him warm while he was injured and trapped on the mountain.

Name_____

Nomads

Maroo's people are semi-nomadic hunters and gatherers. This means that to survive they spend their lives moving from place to place as they forage for food. In the wintertime, they live in the protection of the winter caves and hunt for meat as needed. During the spring, summer, and fall months, they follow the deer on their seasonal migration and gather food. The camps that they live in are temporary and easily relocated. The length of time that they stay in one place depends primarily upon the availability of food.

Although moving offers a certain excitement, the nomadic life is not an easy way to live. Make a list of the positive and negative aspects of living a nomadic life.

Positive	Negative

Would you enjoy following this life style? Explain.

Name _____

Tea

Old Mother prepares hot teas for the family from plants that the children gather. Teas have been made from herbs for centuries. Some people believe that the herbs in teas have medicinal qualities. For example, chamomile tea is said to soothe upset stomachs and mint tea is said to help headaches. Although not everyone believes in the medicinal benefits of herbal teas, it is true that some of the herbs offer vitamins and minerals and that the warmth of the liquid is soothing.

Herbal teas are made by placing either fresh or dried herbs in a pot and then pouring boiling water over the herbs. A cover is placed on the pot, and the mixture is then allowed to sit or steep for 3–5 minutes. The herbs are then strained, leaving a soothing drink. Honey or sugar is often used to sweeten the tea after it has steeped.

Try making some of these herbal teas: mint, chamomile, rose hips, wintergreen, and comfrey. You will need about 1 teaspoon (5 mL) of dried herbs or 1 tablespoon (15 mL) of fresh herbs to 1 cup (250 mL) of water to make each serving of tea. Some of these herbs you may be able to find growing wild in woods near your house. You can also find dried and fresh forms of these herbs at a health food store.

Now, research to find out more about the beliefs surrounding teas. Write what you find here and report your findings to the class.

_____

_____

_____

_____

_____

_____

_____

_____

_____

_____

_____

_____

_____

_____

Name_____

Picture Symbols

Although Maroo's tribe does not have a formalized written language, the members of the tribe make use of picture signs to communicate their ideas. As Maroo's family travels, Slovi leaves messages behind for them in the form of pictures in the sand or carvings in rocks. This helps the family know where to hunt for food or where to find fresh water. Picture communications of this type were the predecessors of our own written language.

In about 3000 B.C., the Egyptians created a form of picture writing that we call hieroglyphics. They continued to use this written form of language until 394 A.D. Through pictures, the Egyptians were able to record stories and important events. Samples of Egyptian hieroglyphics are still studied by scientists today.

Create your own picture symbols for the following words. Then use your symbols to record a message for a friend. Exchange messages and try to decode the picture language.

Word	Symbol		Word	Symbol
I			pizza	
movie			go	
weekend			sleep	
want			house	
eat			homework	
ice cream			work	
like			think	
read			bike	
sports			you	

Make up additional symbols for other words, if you would like.

Challenge:

What words did you have difficulty expressing in picture language? Why do you think this was so? Do you think our written language based on phonics is better or worse than a picture language? Explain your responses on the back of this paper.

Name_____

Traditions

Maroo's tribe bases their lives on many traditions. These traditions have been passed down and honored from one generation to the next. Some traditions have obvious survival values, while others serve the purpose of uniting the community. The traditions provide the foundation for the tribal culture and shape the tribe's way of life.

Read the list of traditions and explain what meaning or purpose each holds for the tribe.

1. "The hunters are modest when asked about their kill."

   _____

2. "Men hunt. Women prepare food."

   _____

3. "The tribe lives together in the winter caves and travels abroad in the summer months."

   _____

4. "The family sings songs and tells stories in the evenings."

   _____

5. "Only women attend the birth of a new child."

   _____

6. "The tribal members make offerings to the spirits."

   _____

7. "The hunters drink the hot blood of their kill."

   _____

8. "The elders in the tribe make the decisions."

   _____

9. "Only men go to the sacred hunters' caves."

   _____

Silent Communication

Instead of talking aloud, the hunters in Maroo's tribe use hand signals while they are hunting. They are able to communicate important information silently without frightening their prey. This skill is necessary for their survival.

Today, American Sign Language is widely used by deaf people nationwide. With this language, people can express themselves by using silent hand movements.

Below are the hand signs for the sign language alphabet as seen by the person reading them. With these letters, you can spell out words to communicate your thoughts. Learn the alphabet and then try to communicate with a partner.

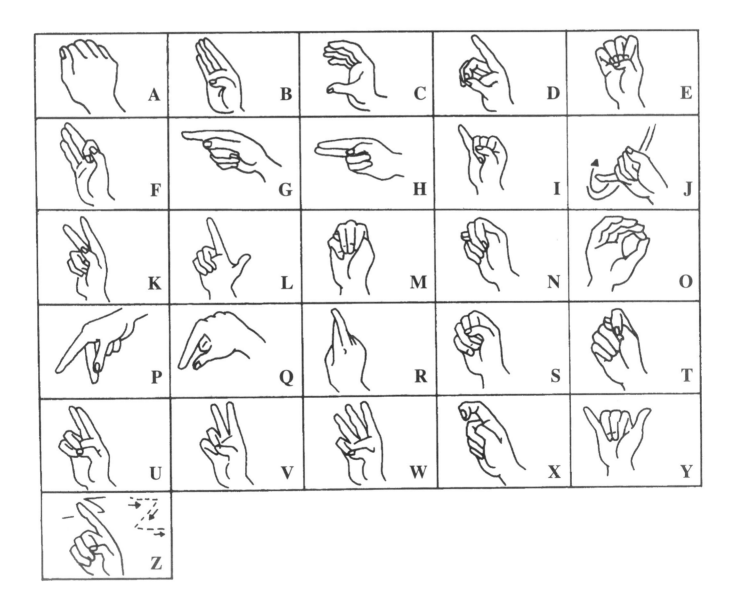

Name_____

Responsibility

There are several situations in the story where Maroo displays her maturity and shows that she is becoming a responsible adult. Old Mother realizes this when she selects Maroo to lead Otak over the mountain for help. How does Maroo show that she is becoming more responsible? Use examples from the novel.

As we mature, we all take on chores or jobs which involve more responsibility. For some of us, maturity brings other changes such as a later curfew or the right to make more of our own choices. What responsibilities have you gained in the last year? How did you show your family that you were ready for these responsibilities? Do you feel that these responsibilities are appropriate for you?

Name_____

Altitude

Maroo and Otak found that they are overwhelmingly exhausted as they near the mountain pass. They feel drained of all strength. Their bodies are most likely affected by the high altitude.

In geography, altitude is defined by measuring the distance a point is above sea level. As the altitude increases, the oxygen level in the air decreases. Our bodies need oxygen in the blood stream to produce energy. Without enough oxygen, our bodies become tired.

Although our bodies need a certain level of oxygen to function, many people have acclimated their bodies to use oxygen more efficiently for better physical performance. After living and training at a higher altitude, a person's body naturally produces more red blood cells to accommodate for the decrease in oxygen. Research has also shown that people who live in the high mountains tend to have larger lungs and faster heart beats. How would larger lungs and a faster heart beat help someone living at a higher altitude?

_____

_____

_____

Many athletes have been known to train at high altitudes. Look at the list of sports. In which sports do you think an athlete could benefit most from training at a higher altitude? Explain your reasoning.

1. cross country skiing_____

2. golf_____

3. boxing _____

4. football_____

5. tennis _____

6. baseball _____

7. soccer_____

8. cycling _____

9. swimming_____

10. figure skating _____

11. downhill skiing _____

12. basketball _____

13. field events _____

14. marathon running_____

15. volleyball _____

Name_____

Self-Preservation

Self-preservation is the instinctive tendency that each of us has to protect ourselves from harm and to ensure our own survival. Although this tendency is a part of each of us, sometimes the decisions that need to be made for self preservation are difficult.

There are several examples of self-preservation in *Maroo of the Winter Caves*. Maroo acknowledges this fact when she states that to survive one must be ruthless, although she realizes that it is important not to risk the loss of more people than necessary in a survival situation.

Read the following quotes from the novel. Respond as to whether you agree or disagree with the decision that is made. Explain why you feel the way you do and what you might have done instead.

Quote	Agree/Disagree	Why?	What would you have done?
1. " 'He would be unwise to wait for us,' Old Mother said."			
2. " 'Maroo and Otak must go alone and fetch help,' Old Mother insisted, 'or we shall all die.' "			
3. "If you need to kill the dog to survive, you must kill him. It will be better to kill him than to take risks hunting larger animals."			
4. "…There must be no risks taken; if one of them was lost or injured, the other must go on. One must survive."			

Name _____

Stories Give You Hope

When Old Mother prepared Maroo and Otak for their journey alone over the mountains, she reminded them to remember the songs and stories. She said, "Stories give you hope, even when the worst comes. A man might have a spear and a full belly, but if he has lost hope, he will die." Explain what Old Mother means by this statement.

_____

_____

_____

_____

_____

_____

_____

_____

_____

_____

_____

Read the story below and discuss how it instills hope. Are there any other stories that you know that help create a feeling of hope?

One day a hare was walking leisurely down the road. He passed by a tortoise who was on her way to visit her brother. The hare, who was a terribly arrogant creature, declared that he could most certainly beat the poky tortoise in a race. The tortoise, who was not interested in racing, said that she did not care to race. The hare became insistent until the tortoise finally agreed, and a time was set for a race the very next day. At the starting line, the hare once again sneered at the tortoise and stated his superiority. When the starting pistol was shot, the hare leapt ahead and was immediately in the lead. The tortoise plodded on at her slow but constant pace. Once the hare rounded the first turn, he paused and decided that since he was so far ahead, he had time to relax for a bit and enjoy the sunshine. He stretched out under a tree and soon feel asleep. Meanwhile, the tortoise continued to plod on along the race course. After much time had passed, the hare awoke to discover that it was late in the afternoon. He leapt to his feet and took off at a full gallop. Just as the hare reached the last stretch of the course, he saw the tortoise cross the finish line. The tortoise turned around and smiled at her amazed opponent standing breathlessly behind her.

Island Survival

Name_____

Creating an Emergency Message

Imagine that you have just been stranded on an island in the South Pacific. There are four of you. You have a radio which can transmit a message for help, but it has limited battery energy. If you are careful, you can transmit one ten-second message. You realize your message will be heard by rescuers, and you want these rescuers to be prepared when they arrive. In this message, you must also give your rescuers some directions to your location. As you look at the island, you can see that it has several distinctive landmarks. To the east there is a volcano. The northern end is rimmed with a beach of deep black sand, and there is a large waterfall to the south. When your ship was destroyed, you know that you were around 15°S latitude and 150°W longitude. You also know that you may have drifted west of this location due to a strong current. One member in your party has broken his leg. Another person is unconscious. Both need medical help immediately.

Create a ten-second message which will both direct your rescuers to your location and ensure that they come prepared for your emergency. Write your message below and then practice it until you can say it clearly in ten seconds.

_____

_____

_____

_____

_____

_____

_____

_____

_____

_____

_____

_____

_____

_____

_____

Constellations

People have been using stars to guide their ways and lives for centuries. Without the use of landmarks, mariners of old depended solely upon compass and stars to direct their ships. Since the stars move in a seasonal fashion, people of ancient times also depended upon the stars to regulate planting and harvesting times. The stars provided ancient people with a compass and a calendar. Since the stars served such an important role for people, names were given to groups of stars to help chart the night sky. We call these star groupings *constellations*. The constellations have been known by many different names by different groups of people. A good example of this is the *Big Dipper*. The Big Dipper is known as the *Bear* by the ancient Greeks, the *Wagon* by the ancient Romans, and the *Plow* by many European people today. To the Hindus, the Big Dipper represents the *Seven Rishis*.

Many of the constellation names were based on ancient stories and myths. The following is a story from Greek mythology which explains the constellation *Cassiopeia*.

Cassiopeia claimed that she was more beautiful than the lovely sea nymphs. The nymphs became angry and complained to Poseidon, god of the sea. Poseidon decided to punish Cassiopeia for her vanity by sending a sea monster to destroy her kingdom. He then demanded that Cassiopeia's daughter be sacrificed to the sea monster in restitution. Fortunately, the young girl was rescued by Perseus before the sea monster could kill her. Cassiopeia was changed into a constellation at her death and was placed into the night sky for all to remember.

Research the names of the following constellations to find their "stories." Share your findings with your class.

- Orion
- Perseus
- Hercules
- Big Bear
- Little Bear
- Pegasus
- Pisces
- Taurus
- Auriga
- Andromeda
- Gemini
- Boötes
- Aquila
- Draco
- Leo

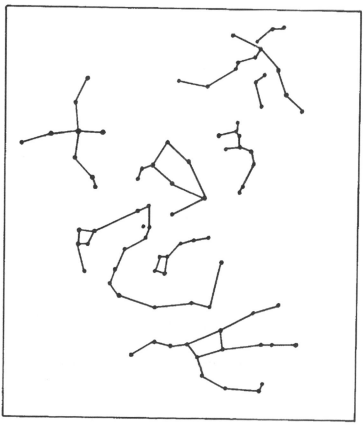

Name_____

Fresh Water

Work in small groups to solve the problem outlined below. Write your solutions in the space provided.

You have been adrift on a raft in the Pacific Ocean for several days. You are suffering from dehydration and hunger. At last you see an island ahead in the sea. You paddle there and land safely, but after a brief inspection of the island, you are unable to find a source of fresh water. You sit down against one of the huge palm trees to think. One of the people from your group brings over some bananas and oranges that she found growing nearby. What do you do to find water so you will not die of dehydration?

Solutions

_____

_____

_____

_____

_____

_____

_____

_____

_____

_____

_____

Fresh Water Solution Experiments

Have students share their answers from the previous page with the class. Make a list of their ideas on the board. Below are a few solutions to this problem.

1. Because many fruits are high in water, fruit from the trees can be used as a water source. Discuss how we can gain water for our bodies through the foods we eat. Try the following experiment.

   Materials: coconuts, bananas, mangos, limes, oranges, a knife, and a glass

   Directions: Cut the fruits and squeeze the juice into a glass. (You will need to tap a hole in the coconut to drain the milk.) Have students measure the amount of fluid each fruit yields. Many of these fruits are over 75% water.

2. Trees need water to survive. If there are trees on the island, there must be a fresh water source to feed the trees. You may be able to tap the underground source by observing where and how the trees grow.

3. Seawater can be evaporated to separate the water from the salt. This method is time consuming and yields little water. (The evaporated water may also still contain some salt if it is heated too quickly.) Try the following experiment.

   Materials: glass flask, hot plate or heat source, pan with a handle, pot holders, and 1 cup (250 mL) seawater (You can make seawater brine by mixing 1 teaspoon [5 mL] salt with 1 cup [250 mL] water.)

   Directions: Place the seawater in the flask and heat to a low boil. When the water is rolling, hold the pan over the opening of the flask. You will trap the steam, and condensation will begin to form on the sides of the pan. Turn the pan over and taste the drops of water in the pan. (Be careful of the heat!) The water should not taste salty.

4. Water can be evaporated from the air and soil by making an evaporation still. This device was designed by Dr. Ray Jackson and Dr. Cornelius H. M. Van Bravel of the U.S. Department of Agriculture. It can yield up to three pints (1.4 L) of water a day.

   Materials: bucket, six-foot (1.8 m) square piece of plastic, rock, shovel

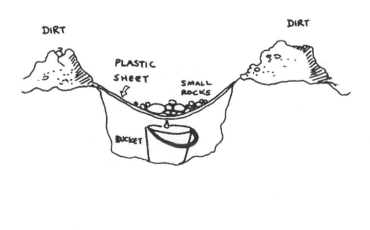

Directions: Dig a hole about 3 feet (90 cm) deep and 3 feet (90 cm) wide in damp soil. Place the bucket in the bottom of the hole. Stretch the plastic sheet over the hole, holding it in place with piles of dirt. (This will seal off the outside air and allow the water to condense under the plastic.) Finally, place a rock in the center of the plastic, weighting it down until it is within 2 inches (5 cm) of the bucket. The trapped water will drip into the bucket. Check on the still the following day.

Locating Directions by the Sun

The sun provides us with a constant directional source and is, therefore, a natural compass. Work in teams to try some of the following methods of locating north, south, east, and west with the use of the sun. Check your results with a compass. When you are finished, make notes about which ways are most accurate. Share your results with the class.

1. **Sun:** The sun rises in the east and sets in the west. Try observing the sun and locating north, south, east, and west. (This method will be more accurate early or late in the day when the sun is not straight overhead.)

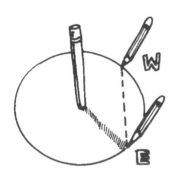

2. **Watch:** If you have a watch that is set to the local time, you can use it as a compass. Hold the watch flat in your hand and then turn the watch until the hour hand is pointing to the sun. If you draw an imaginary line between the hour hand and 12:00, the line will be pointing south.

3. **Stick Shadow:** You will need a flat, sandy location and a short straight stick for this method. (A craft stick would work well.) Push the stick into the ground, angling it toward the sun, so that it will not make a shadow. Wait until it forms a shadow at least 7" (18 cm) long. The shadow that the stick makes will be pointing east. Now you can locate north, south, and west.

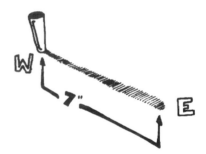

4. **Equal Length Shadow:** You will need a flat, sandy location, two pencils, a yardstick, and a piece of string. In the morning, push the yardstick into the ground. Tie the string with a loose knot at the bottom of the yardstick. Stretch the string out from the yardstick to the end of the yardstick's shadow. Tie the pencil to the string at this point. Use the pencil to sketch a circle in the dirt around the yardstick and then push the pencil into the ground where the shadow meets the circle. In the afternoon, take the second pencil and push it into the ground where the new shadow meets the circle. Sketch a straight line in the dirt to connect the two pencils. This line marks east and west. The morning marker is west. Now you can find north and south.

Locating Directions by the Stars

Since the Earth is constantly revolving around the sun, the location of the stars is always shifting in the sky. Mariners were aware of these changes and learned where stars were located in the skies during all four seasons of the year. Although the location of the stars changes throughout the year, the polestar remains constant. The polestar is the star which is located in the most direct line north over the earth's axis. Since the line of the axis slowly changes over time, the polestar also changes. At this time, the polestar is Polaris, which we also call the North Star. If a navigator is unfamiliar with the seasonal changes of the stars, he or she can always find the North Star to guide the way.

To find the North Star, it is easiest to use the pointers of the surrounding constellations. Use the directions and chart below to locate the North Star in the night sky. Remember that the constellations surrounding the North Star will be aligned differently if you are looking at the sky in a season other than winter.

The North Star is located in the middle of two constellations, the Big Dipper and the Little Dipper. You may have also heard these constellations called Ursa Major and Ursa Minor or Big Bear and Little Bear.

First, locate the Big Dipper in the sky. It is the group of bright stars shaped like a bowl with a handle. Extend an imaginary line through the two stars that make the far side of the bowl. This will point to the North Star. If you follow the North Star up, you will find that it is also the tip of the Little Dipper handle. (Do not be confused by the tail of a faint constellation called Draco the Dragon which falls in between the Big Dipper and the Little Dipper.)

Use the illustration to help you. Once you have found the North Star yourself, try making your own illustration.

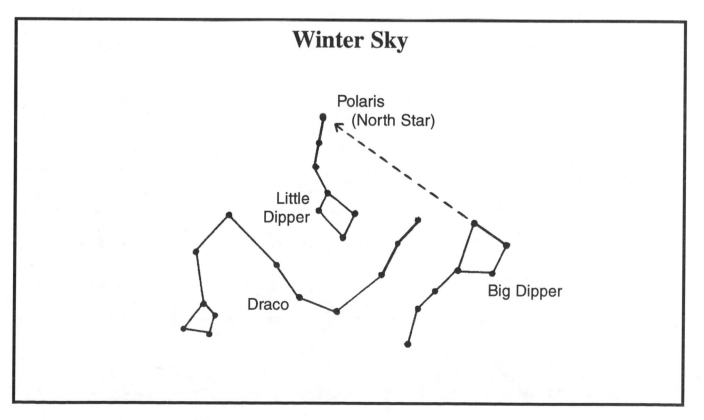

Not Knots!

The common knots that we use today have been around for hundreds of years. Most of them were originally developed by sailors to use on ships. Knot tying was a craft for most sailors. Sailors depended on a number of knots for securing ropes, and they used different knots to perform very specific tasks on their ships. Sailors were constantly inventing new and better methods of tying knots.

Although many of the knots we use today can be attributed to the sailors of hundreds of years ago, the craft of knot tying has been around much longer. Remains of knots over 4,000 years old have been found in Peru. An ancient tribe of Incas in Peru used knots to make fishing nets and ropes strong enough to build suspension bridges.

In ancient folklore, knots were believed to have magical powers. Wizards used them to cast spells or to bring bad luck. In Germany, it was believed that you could get rid of warts by tying knots in a piece of string and then leaving the string under a stone. The first person who stepped on the stone would get the warts, and the person who tied the knots would be rid of them.

Today, knots are especially important to mountain climbers, sailors, and people hiking in the wilderness. The better a knot is tied, the stronger it will be when there is a need for survival. Try tying the knots described on this page and the next. Remember, they are not all easy the first time. Sailors spent hundreds of years developing them!

Bowline

1. Make an overhand loop in the center of a piece of rope.

2. Bring the right end up through the loop.

3. Pass this same piece behind and under the left-hand, straight section of rope.

4. Continue the right-hand piece of rope back down and through the same loop that you passed through in step 2.

5. Tighten the knot by pulling the rope ends.

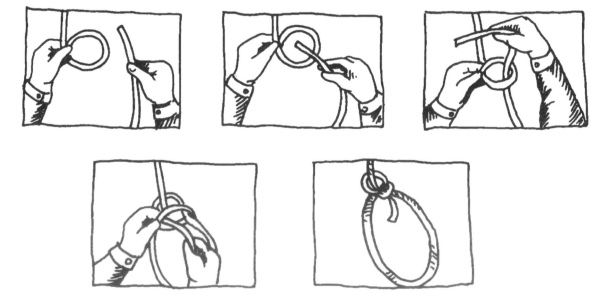

Not Knots! *(cont.)*

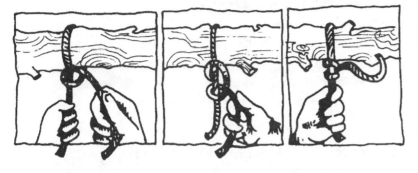

Two Half Hitches

1. Pass the end of the rope around a post. Then pass it over and under the rope facing you. Pull the end through the loop.

2. To make the second half hitch, use your pull rope and repeat the process described in step one.

3. Push the two half hitches together. Tighten by pulling the two rope ends.

Clove Hitch

1. Pass the rope end around a post. Cross the left rope over the right.

2. Pass the right rope end around the post again. Then pass the end of the rope under itself.

3. Tighten the knot by pushing the parts together and pulling on the two rope ends.

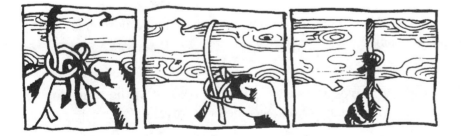

Slip Knot

1. Pass the rope over a post. Loop the right end over and around the left.

2. Pass the right end down through the loop.

3. Tighten the knot by pushing it up against the post and by pulling the left-hand end of the rope down.

Challenges:

1. Can you pick up a piece of rope (holding one end of the rope in each hand) and then tie a knot without letting go of the ends?

2. Can you tie a knot holding the piece of rope behind your back?

Name_____

Sea Measurement

The following are some measurements used by sailors on oceans and waterways. Use these terms to help you answer the word problems below.

> **one fathom** = 6 feet (1.8 m)
>
> **league** = recognized as between 2.4 – 4.6 miles (3.8 – 7.4 km)
>
> **one nautical mile/knot** = 6080.2 feet (about 1.2 miles) per hour (1824.06 m or 1.824 km)

1. A ship is traveling at a rate of 8 knots. How long will it take for this ship to reach an island 20 miles (32 km) away?

    _____

2. A ship is sailing for a destination 10 leagues away. It is traveling at a rate of 5 knots. What is the least amount of time it will take to arrive at the destination? What is the most?

    _____

3. A ship is moored off the coast of an island in water that is 4 fathoms deep. Its hull sits in the water at a depth of 1 fathom. How many feet (meters) of water are between the bottom of the boat and the sea floor?

    _____

4. A submarine is at the surface. It descends 6 fathoms, ascends 3 fathoms, and descends 5 fathoms. How many feet (meters) deep is the sub?

    _____

5. A boat leaves an island at 9:00 AM. It arrives at the next island at 10:00 AM the same day. The islands are 24 miles (38.4 km) apart. How many knots was the boat traveling?

    _____

6. A ship travels 432 miles (691.2 km) in 2 days. The first day it travels for 24 hours at 5 knots. How fast does the ship need to travel to reach its destination by the end of the second day?

    _____

Name_____

Latitude and Longitude

The lines of latitude and longitude are the imaginary lines which are universally accepted as coordinates for locating places on the earth. They are commonly used by people navigating the oceans. The parallels of latitude are the east-west lines which circle the earth, while the meridians of longitude are the north-south lines which circle the earth. Each line is labeled as a degree, and each degree of latitude is separated from the next by approximately 111 kilometers. At the equator, degrees of longitude are also approximately 111 kilometers apart. As they converge at the poles, the longitudinal lines become closer together. Latitudinal lines range from 0° to 90° north and south, while longitudinal lines range from 0° to 180° east and west.

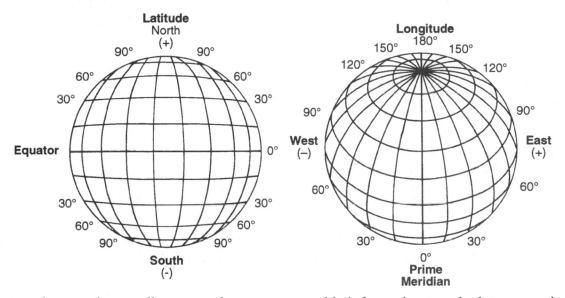

If your map does not have a distance scale, you can use this information to calculate approximate distances. First, locate the latitude or longitude lines which cross a location and then multiply the degrees by 111 kilometers. (Be careful to accommodate your numbers when you cross from north to south at the Equator and from east to west at the Prime Meridian.)

Using the information above and the map on the next page, answer the mathematical problems below.

1. Approximately how many kilometers is it from the Equator to Houston, Texas? _____

2. Approximately how many kilometers long is South America? _____

3. Approximately how many kilometers is it from Venice, Italy, to Cape Town, South Africa?
    _____

4. Approximately how far is it from the coast of Africa to the coast of South America at the Equator? _____

5. Approximately how far is it around the earth at the Equator? _____

6. Find two countries on the map which are approximately 4,995 kilometers apart.

7. Make up five of your own problems using map coordinates and swap with a friend.

Latitude and Longitude *(cont.)*

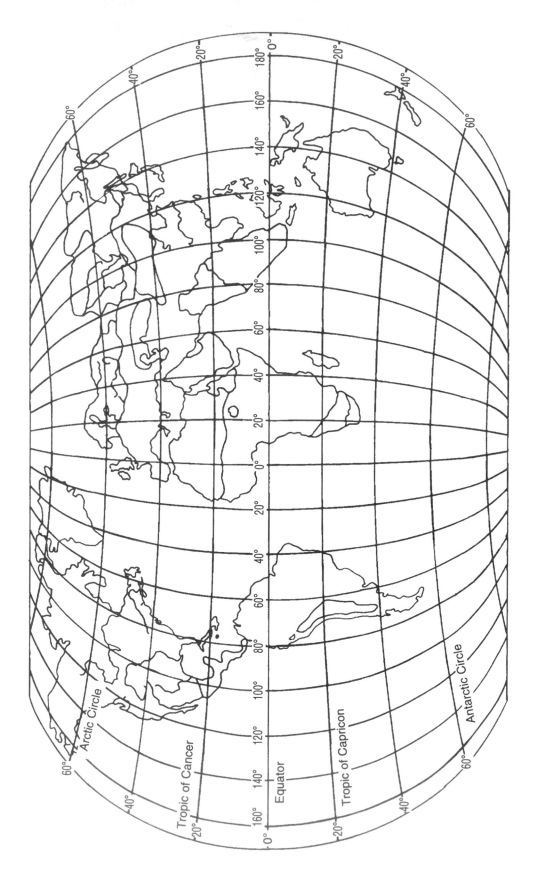

Make Your Own Bowls

On an island, a person can use what is available in nature to make any necessary supplies. For example, practical bowls can be made from coconut shells. Follow these directions to find out how.

Materials:

- ripe coconuts
- hammer
- nail
- knives or carving tools
- saw (an electric table saw is preferable)

Teacher Preparation:

1. Use the hammer and nail to tap two holes in each coconut shell. Drain the milk into a bowl. Save the milk for tasting.

2. Saw the coconuts in half along a line where you made the two holes. (The shells are thick and difficult to saw through with a hand saw. If you have access to a table saw, this process will be much easier.)

3. Rinse the insides of the coconuts.

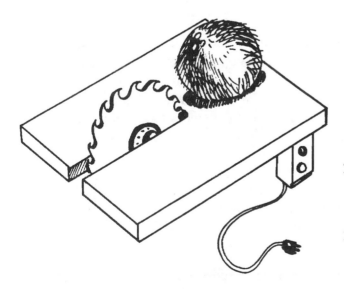

Student Directions:

1. Once you have the coconuts cut in two, the students can begin the scraping work. Have the students use knives to cut the coconut meat away from the hard shell. This works best if they make small cuts into the meat and pry it away from the shell with the knives. Save the meat in a dish to eat raw or to use in the cookie recipe on page 170.

2. When all of the meat is cleaned out of the shell, rinse the inside thoroughly. The coconut shell will now hold water or foods.

3. To smooth and finish the inside of the shell, apply a couple of coats of a non-toxic acrylic varnish designed for non-fired ceramics.

4. Your bowl is ready for use!

Dyes

The ancient art of dyeing was practiced in Egypt, China, and India centuries before the birth of Christ. People were able to enjoy the luxury of producing cloth of multiple colors. Since the chemical dyes of today did not exist, cloth was taken in its raw form and soaked in solutions made from natural ingredients to change its color. These natural dyes were made from sources such as plants, roots, shellfish, berries, and rocks. One such dye was made from a rare mollusk. The purple color that this dye produced was extremely expensive and was worn primarily by royalty.

Today, we have synthetic, or man-made, dyes which are created to represent every color imaginable. We do not need to depend on nature to supply the colors for our cloth. Although chemical dyes are widely available, many people still enjoy the variations that natural dyes have to offer.

Since the colors are not predictable, experimenting with natural dyes can be an interesting art. Use these materials to make some of the natural dyes below. Be sure to follow the directions for mordanting your wool before dyeing, so you will have a colorfast product that will not run in the wash.

Materials:

- glass or stainless steel pot
- stove/burner
- wooden spoon
- 1 pound (500 g) of wool
- mordant
- $^1/_2$ pound (250 g) onion skins (for yellow dye) – $^1/_2$ hour
- $^1/_2$ pound (250 g) tea leaves (for tan dye) – 20 minutes
- $^1/_2$ pound (250 g) ferns (for yellow-green dye) – 2 hours

Wool Preparation:

A mordant acts as a catalyst to join the dye from the plant to the wool or fabric. Alum is a safe, inexpensive, and readily available mordant. To prepare, place 1/3 cup (80 mL) alum and 3 tablespoons (45 mL) cream of tartar in about 4 gallons (15.3 L) water and bring to a boil. Wet 1 pound (500 g) wool in warm water and then place it in the boiling pot of mordant. Lower the burner and allow the wool to simmer for one hour. Squeeze out the excess liquid, and the wool is now ready for dyeing.

Dyeing Directions:

Cover the dye material (onions, tea leaves, or ferns) with water and slowly bring to a boil. Allow to simmer ($^1/_2$ hour for onions, 20 minutes for tea leaves, and 2 hours for ferns). Remove the dye material and add water to fill your pot. Place your damp wool into the pot and slowly bring to a boil. Remove the wool when the desired color is achieved.

Try experimenting with your own ideas. Gather plants, barks, and mosses to make your own dye colors.

Weaving

Weaving has been practiced for over four thousand years in many parts of the world. The old art has been used to produce baskets, fishing nets, tapestries, rugs, carry bags, and an endless array of clothing items. The woven products not only decorate homes, but they also supply people with many useful items which make survival easier.

You do not need a complex loom to create beautiful woven items. Handweaving has been done for centuries without the use of mechanically run looms.

To do your own weaving, follow these directions.

Materials:

- wooden frame at least 12" x 18" (30 cm x 45 cm)
- small-head nails
- hammer
- paint stick at least 2" (5 cm) longer than the width of your frame
- yarn or other weaving material
- table fork
- needle and thread

Frame Directions:

Angle and drive the nails along the top board of the frame, setting them about ¹/₂" (1.5 cm) apart. Drive a second row of nails ¹/₄" (.75 cm) below the first set and place them between each of the nails above creating a staggering effect. Be sure to leave about 2" (5 cm) of clear space on each side of the frame. Repeat at the bottom of the frame.

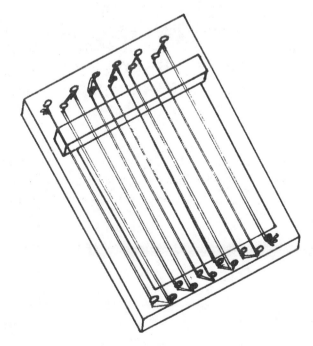

Directions for Warping Your Frame:

Lay the paint stick close to the line of nails at the top of your frame. This will be your tension stick. As you are weaving, the yarn will pull tightly over this stick. When the weave becomes too tight, you can remove this stick, and it will allow you some slack.

To *warp* (string) your frame, tie the end of your yarn to the first top nail on your left. Stretch the yarn to the bottom two corresponding nails and run the yarn behind these nails. Continue this pattern until you have a line of parallel strands ¹/₄" (.75 cm) apart stretched across your frame. When you reach the end, tie off the yarn and cut. Make sure that the yarn is not too tight.

Weaving *(cont.)*

Weaving Directions:

Wind 5' (1.5 m) or so of your yarn into a loose loop, so it can easily pass through the weaving strands. Begin by passing the yarn through the middle strands and weaving over and under until you reach the right edge of the frame. By beginning in the middle, you will have no loose strands on the edges, and the following rows will help hold the first line of weaving in place. Use a table fork to gently push the *weft* (woven strand) to the bottom edge of the frame. Turn your yarn and pass back through the warp. Make sure that you alternate which strands you go over and under in the return pass. Also be sure not to pull your yarn tight at the end but to gently push the yarn into place with your fork as you take up the slack. Continue weaving back and forth until you have about 3" (7.5 cm) of your weft strand

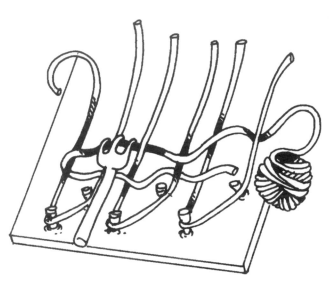

remaining. Pass this to the back of your piece and begin a new strand at the same location. Add new weft strands as needed until you have reached the top of the piece.

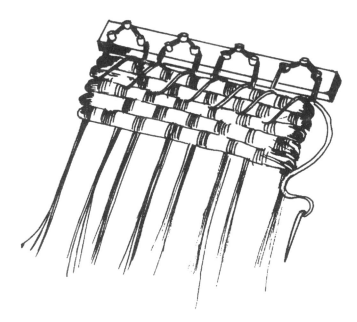

Finishing Directions:

To finish your weaving, take a needle and thread and stitch a row of diagonal stitches across the first two rows and the last two rows of your weaving to keep the rows from slipping. When you slip the weaving off the frame, you can tie the warp strands together, turn them under, or use them to hang and display your weaving.

Outlining a Plan

When you are in a basic survival situation, no matter how well you are prepared, the most important tool you have is your mind. By surveying the situation and organizing your thoughts, you can better cope with the situation. It is best to plan before taking action.

For the following challenge, you will be required to outline a plan before attempting to achieve the task. Read the challenge carefully and work as a team. Good luck!

Set Up:

Measure out a 20-foot (6 m) distance in an open area. Divide the class into cooperative groups of five. Read the challenge described below and then allow the groups time to outline a strategy. After an appropriate amount of planning time, have teams attempt the challenge. Assign points for each portion of the challenge that is completed. Teams may also lose points if they do not follow the restrictions.

Materials:

- tennis racquet
- tennis ball
- blanket
- yard or meter stick
- 5 aluminum pie plates
- box with food items
- large jug filled with water

Challenge:

Your team has just crash landed on the planet Zunad. You know from past missions to the planet that Zunad's surface is composed of a poisonous sand. If any portion of your body comes in contact with the surface, you will become very ill and have to return to the ship to recuperate. Fortunately, you are prepared with zelo discs (pie plates). When you lay these discs on the ground, you can safely step on them. Unfortunately, once the zelo disc is set in the sand, it will remain safe for only seven minutes. Your ship has crashed 30 feet (9 m) from the safety zone. You must move your team and supplies from the ship to the safety zone. You have only 5 zelo discs, and many of your supplies have special protective needs. They are as follows:

1. The water in the jug will evaporate in Zunad's atmosphere after 1 minute of exposure. It will not evaporate on the ship or in the safety zone. (10 points)

2. The food will decompose after 2 minutes of exposure. It will also remain intact in the ship and in the safety zone. (10 points)

3. The blanket must be carried by 3 people. (25 points)

4. The tennis ball is actually an intricate homing device and must be balanced on the head of the tennis racquet at all times so you can be rescued. (20 points)

5. Only 1 person may cross over the sand more than once. (5)

6. You may carry only one item across at a time. (5)

7. Remember, once your zelo discs are set on the surface, you only have 7 minutes before they are of no use.

8. You earn 5 points for every person who makes it safely across.

Call It Courage

by Armstrong Sperry
(Macmillan, 1968)

(Available in Canada and the United Kingdom: Maxwell Macmillan; Australia: Macmillan)

The novel *Call It Courage* is written as a Polynesian folktale. Mafatu is scorned by his people because he is afraid of the sea. He leaves his island to prove his strength and courage to himself and to his people. Once on the open sea, he is tossed by storms and is stranded on a tropical island where he finds food, shelter, and water. He also discovers that the island is one of the forbidden islands and that it is occupied by savages. Mafatu realizes the dangers and begins to build a canoe. While on the island, he saves his dog's life and kills the great shark. He also hunts and kills the wild pig with only a spear. Mafatu develops new skills and finds the strength and courage that he did not have on his home island. When the savages return, Mafatu is driven again to the open sea. He overcomes the ocean and returns to his island village where he surprises his people and is welcomed as a strong, courageous hero.

Name_____

Pacific Island Map

There are hundreds of islands in the Pacific Ocean. When Mafatu leaves his home, he does not know that he will be stranded on one of these strange islands. Do you think Mafatu would have left Hikueru if he had known that he would become stranded? Why or why not?

_____

_____

_____

_____

Would you have left Hikueru?

_____

_____

_____

_____

Name_____

Folklore

Folk means a group of people who have something in common and *lore* means something that is taught or learned. When we discuss folklore and folktales, we are learning about people. Ancient people used songs and storytelling to record their history and to tell about what was important to them. Stories were told over and over again to the younger people in the village so that the stories would not be forgotten. These stories were passed through generations without having been written.

Although much of the folklore we read is fiction, it reflects the people and tells us about issues that were important to them. For example, in the story *Call It Courage*, we know that courage and the sea were very important to the people of the time.

Use the form below to help you write your own folktale. Make sure that your story records or explains some present-day event and that it reflects issues that are important in your community. Remember, folktales are fiction!

Event: _____

Issues: a. _____

           b. _____

           c. _____

Characters: _____

_____

Setting: _____

Plot Summary: _____

_____

_____

_____

_____

_____

Solution/Result: _____

_____

Name_____

Polynesians

The native Polynesians were a strong people. They were tall and robust in stature with an olive-brown complexion and thick, wavy black or brown hair. Today, people who resemble the native Polynesians are spread all over the Pacific from Hawaii to New Zealand.

Although there is some disagreement, most researchers believe that the early Polynesian tribes originally inhabited the Malay Archipelago, a fertile chain of islands surrounding and including New Guinea. In the second century B.C., Malayan invaders drove the Polynesians from this fertile region onto the seas. This scattered the Polynesian people throughout the Pacific and into the island chains that they inhabit today.

The economy of the Polynesians was based primarily on fishing, raising pigs, and gathering fruits. The people were excellent canoe builders and were masters of navigation on the sea. They learned to use both sun and stars to guide their ways. The people depended on plants and wood to make their clothing, tools, and shelters. They were also expert weavers and made rope and cloth from the fibers of plants. Shelters were built with bamboo posts, thatching, and palm leaves. The native Polynesians worshipped animals and natural objects. They believed that nature was full of magical powers.

The Polynesians of old were resourceful and depended greatly on nature to supply them with the tools for survival. Today, technology has touched all corners of the globe. How has this affected the traditions of the Polynesian people? Research in some current magazines and reference books to find out how the Polynesians survive today. Share your information with your classmates.

_____
_____
_____
_____
_____
_____
_____
_____
_____
_____
_____
_____
_____

Name_____

Outcast

In the opening paragraphs of *Call It Courage*, Armstrong Sperry writes the following.

> *There was only courage. A man who was afraid—what place had he in their midst? And the boy Mafatu—son of Tavana Nui, the Great Chief of Hikueru—always had been afraid. So the people drove him forth. Not by violence, but by indifference.*

How does Mafatu feel about his circumstances? Does he have a choice?

_____

_____

_____

_____

_____

_____

_____

_____

Think of someone in your community whom you consider to be an outcast. Why does this person not "fit in"? Is this person an outcast by choice? Could this person change his/her status as an outcast? How?

_____

_____

_____

_____

_____

_____

_____

_____

_____

Name_____

Courage

What is courage? To some, it represents strength and power. To others it represents self-control and calm. Mafatu assesses his own courage as he prepares to return to Hikueru. He notes that he survived with his own wits and skills. He faced loneliness, danger and death, and although he was sometimes deeply afraid, he faced his fear and won. Mafatu's courage represents both strength and calm.

Use this space to describe someone whom you feel is courageous.

_____

_____

_____

Courage is the core of tradition for the people of Hikueru. Describe what courage means to the people of Hikueru.

_____

_____

_____

Find examples in the text which show courage for each of these characters.

1. Mafatu's mother_____

_____

2. Tavana Nui_____

_____

3. Kana_____

_____

4. Mafatu _____

_____

5. Uri _____

_____

Name_____

Companionship

When Uri falls off the raft and is almost attacked by the hammerhead shark, Mafatu is moved to dive into the water to save his dog. After he kills the shark and pulls the dog to safety, he hugs the animal close and talks to him foolishly. Mafatu risks his life to save the dog. Why is Uri's companionship so important to Mafatu?

Imagine that you are stranded on an island. Who would you choose to be your companion? Use the space below to explain why. Share your response.

_____

_____

_____

_____

_____

_____

_____

As a follow-up to your discussion, try this activity. If your desks are situated in groups, move each desk so it has no contact with another. As individuals, imagine that you are alone on separate islands. You have no way to communicate with anyone in the room. Attempt to spend the entire day without speaking to or recognizing the people who surround you. During this time, write down your thoughts about what you are feeling. Then, answer this question: Is companionship important to survival? Explain.

_____

_____

_____

_____

_____

_____

_____

_____

Name_____

Translation Puzzle

There are many native words from Mafatu's language throughout the text of *Call It Courage*. Use your book to help you translate the words and solve the crossword puzzle.

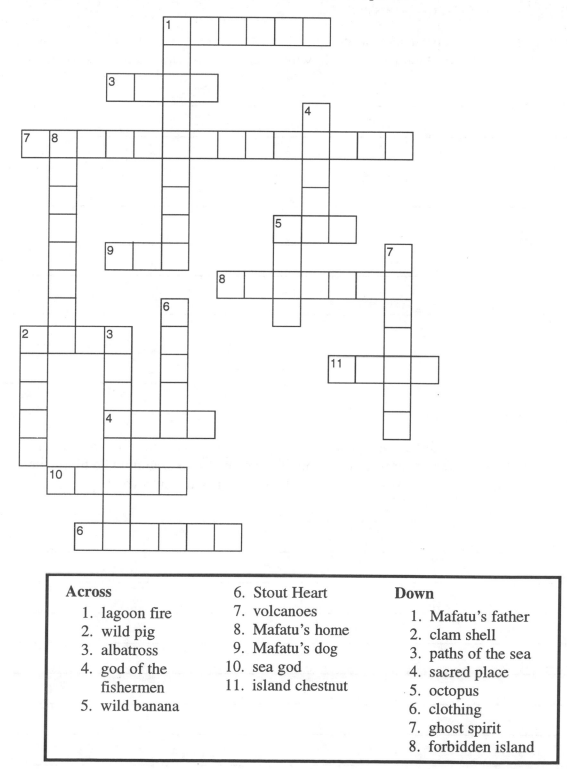

Across

1. lagoon fire
2. wild pig
3. albatross
4. god of the fishermen
5. wild banana
6. Stout Heart
7. volcanoes
8. Mafatu's home
9. Mafatu's dog
10. sea god
11. island chestnut

Down

1. Mafatu's father
2. clam shell
3. paths of the sea
4. sacred place
5. octopus
6. clothing
7. ghost spirit
8. forbidden island

Name_____

Trophies

Mafatu returns to Hikueru with several trophies. A trophy is something that is gained in a victory or conquest, and it often holds some personal value for an individual. A trophy does not have to be a golden cup or a plaque mounted on a stand.

Each of Mafatu's trophies represents an accomplishment for Mafatu. Explain what each of the following trophies means to Mafatu and explain why he chooses to bring them back to Hikueru.

1. bone knife _____

_____

2. canoe _____

_____

3. boar's teeth_____

_____

4. spear_____

_____

5. octopus tentacle _____

_____

We all have trophies that remind us of special accomplishments. Sometimes the trophy can be as simple as a T-shirt earned for participation in a tennis match or a rock found while hiking an especially tall mountain. What are some of your trophies, and what do they mean to you?

_____

_____

_____

_____

_____

_____

_____

Name_____

Polar Opposites

Read the statements listed below. Then choose the number ratings which you think most accurately complete the statements. Be prepared with examples from the story to support your choices.

1. Uri is a/an _____ dog.

1	2	3	4	5
faithful				unfaithful

2. In the beginning of the story, Mafatu is _____.

1	2	3	4	5
brave				cowardly

3. The boys in the village are _____to Mafatu.

1	2	3	4	5
cruel				kind

4. Mafatu learns _____while stranded on the island.

1	2	3	4	5
much				little

5. Water _____ a concern to Mafatu.

1	2	3	4	5
is				is not

6. Mafatu feels _____ on the island.

1	2	3	4	5
safe				unsafe

7. The villagers are _____ when Mafatu returns.

1	2	3	4	5
proud				embarrassed

Extensions:

1. Get together with a team of three or more students to share your responses and their supports from the book.

2. Choose one or more of the statements from above and write a paragraph explaining why you chose the number rating. Include examples from the book to support your reasoning.

3. Write five of your own polar opposite statements to accompany the story.

Island of the Blue Dolphins

by Scott O'Dell
(Dell Publishing, 1960)

(Available in Canada: Doubleday Dell Seal; the United Kingdom: Doubleday Bantam Dell; Australia: Transworld Publications)

Based on the true story of an Indian girl who was found on an island off the coast of California in the early 1800s, *Island of the Blue Dolphins* is an amazing story of survival. When Karana and her brother, Ramo, are digging roots on the far side of the island, they see a ship sailing into the harbor. This ship has brought Aleut hunters. The captain of the Aleut ship strikes a deal with Chief Chowig so he can camp on the island and hunt otter. Unfortunately, the captain of the Aleuts is not true to his word, and he attempts to leave the island without paying for the otter he and his men have killed. In a battle on the beach, many of the men from the island tribe are killed, and the Aleuts flee with the otter. Following this massacre, the island tribe is depressed. Their men are dead, and the island is heavy in spirit. One of the remaining men, Kimki, decides to leave the island in search of another island. After almost a year, Kimki returns in a ship and is prepared to take the entire tribe to a new home. The tribe anxiously packs and boards the ship. As the ship starts for the open sea, Karana realizes that her brother is not on board. She jumps into the sea and swims to the shore. Since the ship is unable to turn around, Kimki calls that he will send a ship soon to rescue them from the island. The next day, Karana's brother is killed by a pack of wild dogs, and Karana is left alone on the island. While she waits for Kimki to return, she collects food, builds a house, and creates weapons to protect herself. She does not know that the ship carrying her tribe was destroyed in a storm and that there were no survivors. Instead, Karana lives in the hope of being rescued.

During the following eighteen years on the island, Karana becomes self-sufficient. She receives companionship by taming the animals with whom she lives, she hunts and prepares for winter, and she watches for the return of the Aleut hunters. When Karana is finally discovered by missionaries eighteen years after being left on the island, she is a grown woman and the sole survivor of her tribe.

Name_____

Coastal Map

Saint Nicholas Island is one of several islands off the coast of Southern California. History tells us that although it was settled by Indians in 2000 B.C., it was unknown to Spanish explorers until 1602. The Indian inhabitants of the island were left relatively undisturbed until around 1835.

Locate San Nicholas Island, or the "Island of the Blue Dolphins," on the map. Use the scale to calculate about how far it is to the surrounding islands and to the California coast. Then, on the back of this paper, respond to this question: Do you think the isolation of this island affected the inhabitants in a positive or a negative way?

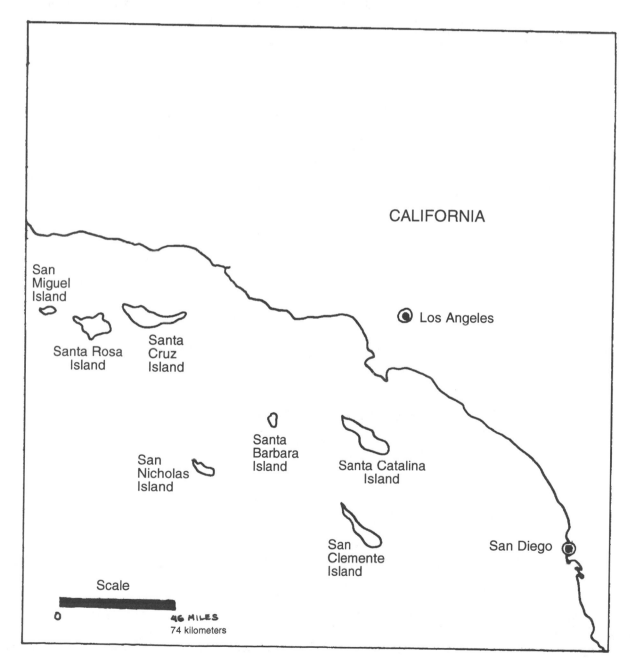

Name _____

Mapping Descriptions

Knowing your surroundings is important for survival. Without a clear picture of an area, an individual may limit or be unaware of important resources. Mapping out a region can help one organize and remember where important landmarks are for future use.

Most of the maps that we use are diagrams rather than pictures. This means that the map maker has used symbols to represent mountains, lakes, rivers, and other landmarks instead of actual pictures. The reader can identify these symbols by referring to the map's key or legend.

Karana describes her island early in the novel. Read Karana's description and design a map of the island in the space provided below. As you continue to read the story, add details to your map describing the places that Karana frequents throughout her years on the island. You can develop your own symbols to represent the landmarks. Be sure to record all of your symbols in a key so anyone reading your map will understand their meanings.

The Island of the Blue Dolphins

Name_____

Sex Roles

Within Karana's tribe, the men and women had clearly defined roles. The men defended the island, hunted for food, and built canoes, while the women gathered roots, made clothing, and cooked. Since the work was divided equally, the tribe survived in peace. The traditions of these roles were so ingrained in the people that they became tribal law. Superstition even surrounded the following of these laws. Karana had been told that if she were to make a weapon, the weapon would break in a time of dire need and danger.

Although we live in a society which is much more liberal than Karana's, many of us still have roles within our families which are performed by either the males or the females. What roles do you have in your family? Are there certain jobs that only the males or females do in your house? Do you agree with these roles? What would happen if you were to go against these roles?

Make a list of the jobs in your home and who usually performs them. Write beside each whether you agree or disagree with the role assignment and explain your reasoning.

Job	Who Performs	Agree/Disagree	Why?

Name_____

Bravery

Although she is but a young girl with little survival experience outside her tribal community, Karana is brave and accomplishes what is necessary to survive alone on the island.   One of the greatest examples of her bravery occurs when she realizes that her brother is left behind on the island, and she leaps into the stormy ocean so he will not be abandoned alone. Through this action, she not only shows her courage, but she also unknowingly saves her own life.

Read the acts of bravery listed below. Explain Karana's motivation behind attempting to accomplish each act.

1. leaping into the ocean to be with her brother on the island _____

_____

2. killing the wild dogs _____

_____

3. saving the lead wild dog's life and taming him_____

_____

4. crossing the ocean alone in a canoe to be with her tribe_____

_____

5. attempting to kill the bull sea elephant _____

_____

6. making friends with Tutok_____

_____

7. entering the Black Cave_____

_____

8. attacking the devil fish_____

_____

Answer:

Do you think you would have been able to accomplish these feats and survive as Karana does?

_____

_____

Endangered Species

In the mid 1800s, the fur trade was thriving. Hunters up and down the West Coast were trapping and trading furs for goods. Demand for precious furs was high. Unfortunately, the sea otter was one of the animals prized for its pelt. Hunters traveled from Alaska to Southern California to capture the furs. As a result, the playful sea otters were hunted almost to extinction by the late 1800's. Since then, the government has taken an interest in sea otters and has placed a ban on the hunting of these creatures. Although there are still hunters who illegally poach these animals for their fur, the population of sea otters off the coast of California is increasing.

Many other species have suffered the same massacre as the sea otters. Choose one of the endangered animals listed below to research. Find out where it lives, what perils it has survived, and how many still exist. Share this information with your classmates.

- whooping crane
- ivory-billed woodpecker
- mongoose lemur
- giant anteater
- dwarf gibbon
- sperm whale
- blue whale
- red wolf
- black-footed ferret
- snow leopard
- Mediterranean monk seal
- Amazonian manatee
- Sumatran rhinoceros
- marsh deer
- red deer
- giant armadillo

You may wish to write to one of the following organizations to learn more about wildlife protection.

National Wildlife Foundation 1400 16th Street NW Washington, DC 20036 (202)637-3700	**World Wildlife Fund** 1250 24th Street NW Washington, DC, 20037 (202)293–4800

Animal Rights

There are many groups in the United States which have opposing views on animal rights. For example, the American Medical Association believes that animal experimentation is a benefit to human health because it allows researchers to develop new drugs and techniques that save human lives. The Humane Society disagrees with this premise. This organization believes that animal experimentation is not necessarily a benefit to human health because the results of the experiments are not always directly related to humans. Both groups have arguments based on facts to support their views.

How do you feel about animal rights? Hold your own series of debates in your classroom to further explore animal rights. Several debatable issues are listed below. Divide the class into cooperative teams. Assign an argument for each team to research. Remember, a good debate is based on fact, not opinion. Once the teams are ready, allow each team to present its views. Be sure to allow equal time for each team to present its ideas. The class can vote to decide which team presented a more convincing argument.

Issues

1. A. Zoos are a benefit to animal populations.

    B. Zoos are not a benefit to animal populations.

2. A. Animal experimentation in laboratories should be allowed.

    B. Animal experimentation in laboratories should not be allowed.

3. A. Hunting animals should be allowed.

    B. Hunting animals should not be allowed.

4. A. Trapping animals for fur is justified.

    B. Trapping animals for fur is not justified.

Teacher Note: You may want to write the issues on slips of paper and have teams randomly choose, or you may have students group together by selecting topics that interest them.

Name_____

Loneliness

Karana spends eighteen years alone on her island. During this time, her sole companions are Rontu and the other animals she tames. When the Aleuts return to the island and Karana meets Tutok, she remembers what it is like to talk with a human. She enjoys the companionship and sharing. After Tutok leaves, Karana thinks of her people and the hope of once again meeting them.

We have all felt lonely at one time or another. How does it feel to be lonely? Do you have to be alone to feel lonely?

Use the web format to brainstorm words that have to do with loneliness. The word "loneliness" is written in the center for you.

(**loneliness**)

Now use your word bank to write a poem expressing your feelings about loneliness.

Name_____

Responsibilities

Karana's life and responsibilities change dramatically when she is left to survive on the island alone. She no longer has her family or village to support and protect her. She must accomplish the jobs of all the village by herself if she wishes to survive.

As you are reading *Island of the Blue Dolphins*, make notes about typical responsibilities in Karana's life during her isolation. Give specific examples from the text to support your ideas. Beside each chore, make a note explaining who would have typically completed this chore if Karana had not been alone.

Responsibilities	Who?

Name_____

Languages

Language is the means by which we communicate with one another. It is the transmission of thoughts and ideas through words, print, and gestures. Without language, our thoughts have no meaning to others.

When Karana meets Tutok, they share many happy hours learning words and ideas from one another's languages. They even find that some of their words are very similar. We call words that are similar in two or more languages "cognates."

Read the words and phrases below. Work in teams to research and find out how they are said in the languages listed. If you are already familiar with some of the languages, share your knowledge with your classmates. The blank spaces are left for you to add some words of your own choosing.

Word	English	Spanish	French	American Sign	Chinese	Your Language Choice
1. mother						
2. father						
3. hello						
4. good-bye						
5. friend						
6. school						
7. My name is ( ).						
8. What is your name?						
9. I am hungry.						
10. Where is the bathroom?						
11.						
12.						

War Survival

Name_____

Morse Code

Today, we commonly use telephones when we want to transmit a message over a long distance. However, before the use of telephones, other means of communication were utilized. Messages were often sent on paper. More urgent messages may have been sent by Morse code.

Morse code is a system of dashes and dots. Each combination of dashes and dots represents a different letter in the alphabet. Samuel Morse developed this language in 1835 to send messages over long distances with a telegraph machine. Morse code is still commonly used in emergencies by people today when telephone services are interrupted or unavailable.

You can use a flashlight, a whistle, a buzzer, or a light reflective mirror to transmit a Morse code message. Use the code to create a message for a friend. Then use one of the suggested methods for transmission to send your message. Challenge your friend to decode your message.

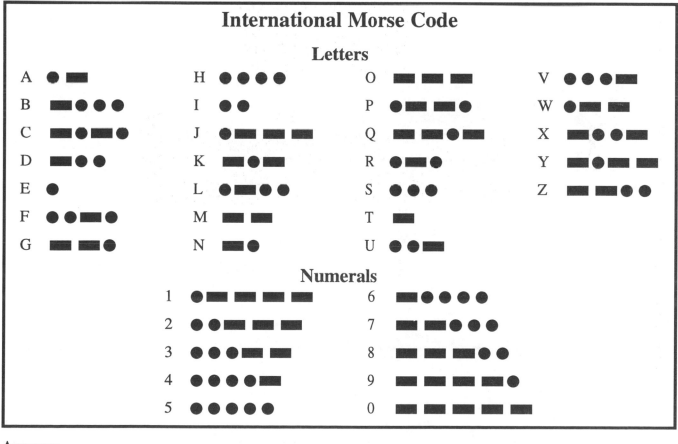

Answer:

What are some of the benefits of Morse code? _____

_____

What are some of the drawbacks of Morse code? _____

_____

Name_____

Public Services

In times of war, normal government-run public services are usually interrupted. The electricity, gas, and water service may be erratic, and organizations such as the police force, fire department, and waste disposal services may be unavailable.

Think about the public services that you may take for granted yet depend upon in your daily life. Make a list of these services.

Public Services

Respond:

How would your life change without each of these services?

_____

_____

_____

_____

Name _____

Power of the Press

Even after having its main office and its printing press destroyed by mortar attacks, a newspaper in Sarajevo continued to print a weekly one-page newspaper for the citizens still living in the city. For some, this paper was the only news source available. When electricity failed and people could not watch television or listen to the radio, the newspaper could be read.

Why do you think the reporters and press operators risked their lives by going to work through sniper fire just for a one-page paper?

_____

_____

_____

_____

_____

_____

_____

_____

All over the world, reporters risk their lives daily to report the news. Over the next couple of weeks, watch the national news. Note how many people are reporting news from dangerous places. How do the reports that these people deliver impact our lives?

_____

_____

_____

_____

_____

_____

_____

_____

_____

Name_____

Water Purification

The water that we drink out of the tap has been through many purification processes to make it safe to drink. Scientists have filtered the water and have added chemicals such as chlorine to kill bacteria, sodium sulfite to enhance the taste, and fluoride to improve our teeth. All drinking water is required to pass purification guidelines established by the U.S. Public Health Service before it reaches our homes.

Water found in a stream or lake in the wilderness is often filled with micro-organisms such as giardia that can make us sick. Before consuming any water in the wilderness, you should purify it to make sure that it is safe to drink. Here are a few common ways to purify water before drinking it:

- **Boiling:** By boiling water you can kill the organisms that might harm you. Be sure that the water is brought to a rolling boil for at least three minutes.

- **Filters:** Water filter systems can be purchased that strain out the micro-organisms. These pumps work by sucking the water through microscopic pores. The pores trap the micro-organisms and allow the water molecules to pass.

- **Iodine:** Iodine tablets can be added to water to kill the micro-organisms. These tablets change the flavor of the water but make it safe to drink.

  Note: Freezing water *will not* kill all micro-organisms.

Activity:

Bring in some samples of water to observe under a microscope. Does the water out of your school's tap look different from the water from a local stream or a mud puddle? Record your observations below.

Water Observations

Try some of the water purification methods on your samples. Do any of these methods change how the water samples look under a microscope?

Survival Kits

Being prepared in an emergency situation is the first step to survival. A survival kit can help provide you with the tools you will need.

Discuss unpredictable emergency situations such as floods, earthquakes, or tornadoes with your class. (You may live in an area where some of these emergencies commonly occur.) Ask your students about the benefits of being prepared for an emergency. Discuss the purpose of making a survival kit and where you might store it for easy access in an emergency situation.

Tell students that they will be putting together their own survival kits with items from school and home. Remind them that the kits need to be small and light so the boxes they bring in should be about the size of a shoe box.

To start your students brainstorming about what should go into their kits, write "Survival Needs" on the board. Under this you can write "food," "water," "clothing," and "shelter." Ask the students to list items that they could place in their kits to meet these needs. Have students take home their lists and begin gathering items to make their kits.

Here is a list of items that you might wish to include in the survival kits:

• compass	• sealed water bottle
• iodine tablets	• rope
• dehydrated food	• flashlight with fresh batteries
• pocket knife*	• paper and pencil
• matches in an airtight plastic bag*	• lightweight space blanket
• candle	• basic first aid kit (enclosed in a clean, sealed plastic bag)**

*Students may not be allowed to bring these items to school, but they may choose to place them in their kits when they store them at home.

**The contents of a basic first aid kit are the following:

• bandages	• disinfectant
• roll tape	• first aid cream
• band-aids	• small scissors
• needle and thread	• list of emergency numbers

When the kits are complete, students can decide where they will keep them for future emergency use. Students' completed kits would also make an interesting display on a survival theme night. (See pages 169–171)

Basic First Aid

It is important in any emergency or survival situation to follow basic fist aid procedures. It is wise for everyone to know these rules and techniques.

Remain Calm: When treating someone who is injured, try to remain calm. If you are calm, it will help the victim also remain calm.

Survey the Situation: Before beginning any treatment, always take a quick look at the situation. You may be able to learn more about what is wrong, and you will ensure that it is safe for you to help.

Poisoning: If you suspect that someone has swallowed something poisonous, immediately call the poison control center or the emergency services in your town. Tell the dispatcher exactly what the victim swallowed. Wait for instructions.

Shock: Any person who has been badly injured is likely to go into shock. This means that the body is shutting down and is depressing its normal functions. While waiting for emergency help to arrive, you can maintain the victim's body temperature by wrapping him or her in a blanket. If the person has no head or facial injuries, it is often helpful to lie the person down and elevate his or her feet 8–10 inches (20–25 cm). Try to keep the person calm.

Cuts and Scratches:

Direct Pressure: You can usually control bleeding by placing a bandage over the wound and pressing firmly with the palm of your hand.

Elevate: If the injury does not involve broken bones, you can also lift the wounded limb higher than the victim's heart.

Breaks and Sprains:

If you can wait for emergency services to arrive, it is best not to move the person. This will ensure that the break does not become more severe. You can treat this person for shock.

If you are not able to call or send for help, you can immobilize the limb by using a splint. (Always try to splint the limb as it lies. Do not move it. If you move a broken limb, it may worsen the situation.)

1. Place two stiff, well-padded splints on each side of the limb. You can use sticks, newspaper, cardboard, or any straight, stiff material to make your splint.

2. Use bandages, cord, or cloth to secure the splint in place. Tie the splint in several places so the limb cannot move. Do not tie a knot directly over the break.

Activities:

1. Make up injury scenarios and have students role play the situations.

2. Have students practice splinting techniques by referring to a first aid book.

Emergency Response

Knowing what to do in an emergency may save a life. It is a good idea to practice some basic first aid skills so that you will be prepared. Review the following information with your students. Then, do the activity.

Emergency Phone Call:

Whenever a victim is in a life-threatening situation, you should always call for help. Many communities have access to emergency services by calling 911. This number will connect you to a dispatch person who can transfer your call. If your community does not have a 911 service, you can dial 0 for the operator, or dial your local hospital or fire station directly.

When you make an emergency call, you should always give the following information:

1. Give your name and the phone number from where you are calling. This will help the dispatcher if your phone line is disconnected.

2. Give the address and location of the emergency. This information will be routed to the emergency service people.

3. Describe the accident. This will help the dispatcher decide what emergency services may be required and what they should be prepared for.

Activity:

Have your students practice making emergency phone calls. Write brief descriptions of emergency situations on slips of paper and have your students select them from a hat. Pair students with partners and have them take turns being the dispatcher and the emergency caller. Have a couple of students model their conversations in front of the class.

The following are some resources that you may want to tap for further instructional materials or information.

National Safety Council
444 N. Michigan Avenue
Chicago, Illinois 60611
(312) 527–4800

National Injury Information Clearinghouse
5401 Westbard Avenue
Room 625
Washington, DC 20207
(301) 492–6424

Your Local Red Cross Chapter

Also worthwhile is the publication entitled *American Red Cross Advanced First Aid and Emergency Care* produced by the American Red Cross and published by Doubleday & Company in 1979.

Teacher Note: You may want to invite a health professional to instruct your class in further first aid techniques such as rescue breathing, airway obstruction, and CPR.

Name_____

Blockades and Embargoes

The objective of a blockade is to close all foreign commerce to a country or region. By blocking the passage of goods, the military inside the country is denied supplies and outside communications. Without supplies, the military cannot support itself.

An embargo contributes to the success of the blockade. When an embargo is imposed upon a country, the country is prohibited from exporting goods outside the country's borders. This means that the country can no longer gain any monetary benefits from its goods.

Blockades and embargoes are frequently used as a passive way to coerce a country into making changes. Blockades in recent years have been imposed on Iraq during the war in Kuwait and in Cuba to change the policies of the acting government.

Although blockades and embargoes are designed to hurt the military, the civilians in the country are often the ones who suffer. Not only is the military denied supplies, but so are the civilians. Food, fuel, and medical supplies often become scarce, and in many cases, the supplies that are available are saved for military use.

How effective are blockades and embargoes? Research to find out how effective blockades and embargoes have been in recent history. Then use this information to argue for or against the use of this military strategy. Summarize your ideas below.

_____

_____

_____

_____

_____

_____

_____

_____

_____

_____

_____

_____

Name_____

Community

Acts of war or crisis often serve to bring a community of people closer together. Resources may be scarce and transportation limited. It is often through community cooperation that people are able to survive.

How well do you know your community and the people who live there? Research to find the answers to these questions about your community.

1. Who are your neighbors?_____

_____

_____

2. What special talents do your neighbors have? _____

_____

_____   _____

3. How is your community unique?_____

_____

_____

4. How well is your community prepared for an emergency? _____

_____

_____

5. How and by whom was your community founded? _____

_____

_____

6. What are the major industries and resources in your community?_____

_____

_____

Share these facts about your community with your classmates.

Name_____

Percentages

A family is trying to assess how much food is still available after a bomb struck the kitchen and almost destroyed the refrigerator. Separate the foods into the six major food groups. Then, find the percentage of the total food belonging to each food group left in the refrigerator and fill in the pie graph.

- milk 32 oz.
- corn 9 oz.
- bread 9 oz.
- cereal 4 oz.
- broccoli 16 oz.
- cheese 3 oz.
- oranges 2 oz.
- hamburger 1 oz.
- artichokes 7 oz.
- ice cream 2 oz.

- apples 8 oz.
- chicken 18 oz.
- chocolate bar 13 oz.
- fish 12 oz.
- bananas 4 oz.
- yogurt 6 oz.
- tomatoes 9 oz.
- flour 16 oz.
- grapes 3 oz.

To solve: Add the total amount of ounces. Then add the ounces in each food group. Divide the total ounces into each food group total. Multiply the answers by 100 to find the percentages. You may round your answers to the nearest whole number.

Dairy   =_____ %

Grains   =_____ %

Fruits   =_____ %

Vegetables   =_____ %

Meats   =_____ %

Fats   =_____ %

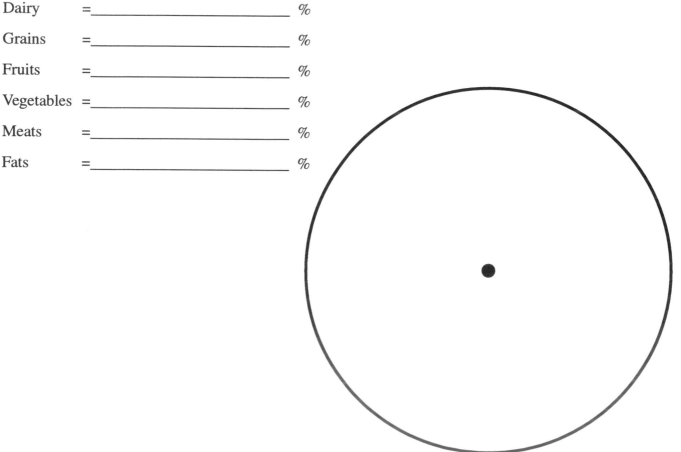

Name_____

Roadblock Logic

The town of Freedom has just gone to war with the town of Harmony. Since the towns have always been friendly in the past, they have shared the same bakery, grocery store, swimming pool, gas station, and laundromat. Now, with the fighting and roadblocks, it is more difficult for the citizens in the towns to access the services they always used. The Hate River splits the two towns.

Use the town map to solve these problems. Answer on the back or a separate piece of paper.

1. Sara wants to go to the laundromat. What are her route options?

2. Paige needs to get gas for her pickup. What route will take Paige on the fewest streets?

3. Michelle needs to buy bread at the bakery. She would also like to stop to see how her friend, Rachel, has been doing since the war started. What route should she take?

4. How many ways can Chris get to Paige's house?

5. Without backtracking on a road that he has already traveled, how many ways can Eli get to the grocery store?

6. What is the most direct route for Fritz to get to the swimming pool?

7. Kathleen wants to meet Chris for lunch. What are her route options?

8. Hannah and Tom need to do laundry. What is the most direct route to the laundromat for each?

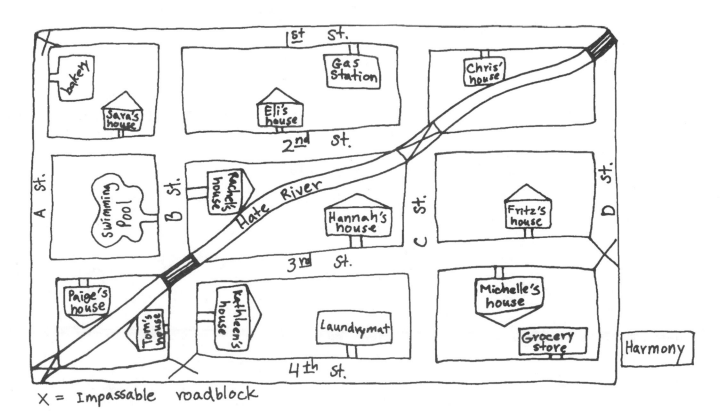

X = Impassable roadblock

Name_____

Peace Symbol

This recognized symbol of peace was introduced by Lord Bertrand Russell in 1958 when he was campaigning for nuclear disarmament in England. It actually stands for worldwide nuclear disarmament. Most people agree that the symbol is based on the semaphore alphabet (an alphabet based on positioning two flags to represent each letter). The letter N (for nuclear) is represented by holding two flags down at an angle at one's side. The letter D (for disarmament) is represented by holding one flag straight down and one flag straight up. The circle means worldwide, or total.

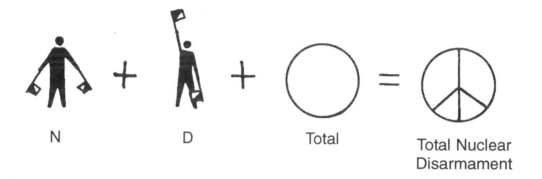

N   D   Total   Total Nuclear Disarmament

If you were to design your own symbol of peace, what would it look like? Use the space below to design a peace symbol. Then, write a paragraph explaining what the symbol means to you.

Capture the Flag

The game called Capture the Flag involves two opposing teams. Each team has a fort with a flag. The goal of the game is to capture the other team's flag and to bring it back to the fort.

Materials:

- large playing field
- two flags
- marking tape, cones, or chalk
- optional: individual tag flags

Set Up:

Draw a line down the center of the playing field. Set a fort and a jail for each team at each end of the field. (To do this, mark off two 4' [1.2 m] square areas at each corner of the field.) Place a flag in each fort. (If you do not have many players, the fort and jail can be combined.)

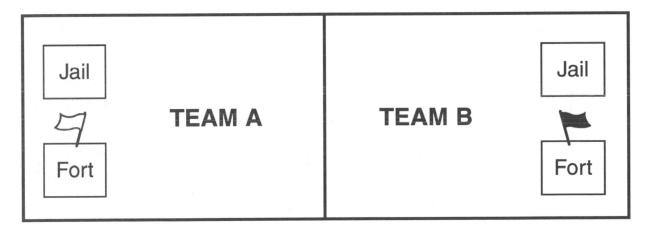

General Rules:

Divide the class into two teams. Assign team A to one end of the playing field and team B to the other. The field between team A's fort and the center line is considered safe for team A, and the space between team B's fort and the center line is safe for team B. Once a member of team A crosses into team B's territory, he or she can be captured and taken to team B's jail and vice-versa. The goal is for each team to cross safely into enemy territory and capture the opposing team's flag. The team members must then attempt to bring it safely back to their own fort.

Capture:

To capture an opposing team member, he or she must be tagged. The prisoner must then be escorted to the jail where he or she will wait until there is a jailbreak. (If each person is wearing a team color-coded flag, to capture someone the flag must be pulled loose.)

Jail:

Once there are people trapped in the jail, the opposing team can attempt a jailbreak to free their team members. To do this, at least three team members have to arrive safely in the jail and yell, "Free! Free! Free!" The prisoners may then walk safely back to their own side and then resume play.

Capture the Flag *(cont.)*

Safe Territory:

Each member is safe on his or her team's side of the playing field. Each person is also safe once he or she enters either team's fort or jail. The exception is when a flag is removed from a fort. Once a flag is taken, the individual carrying the flag is not safe until he enters his or her own fort.

Strategy:

It is often helpful to set a team strategy. Guards are usually set at both the forts and the jails, and team members plan together to free one another and to move the flag down the field.

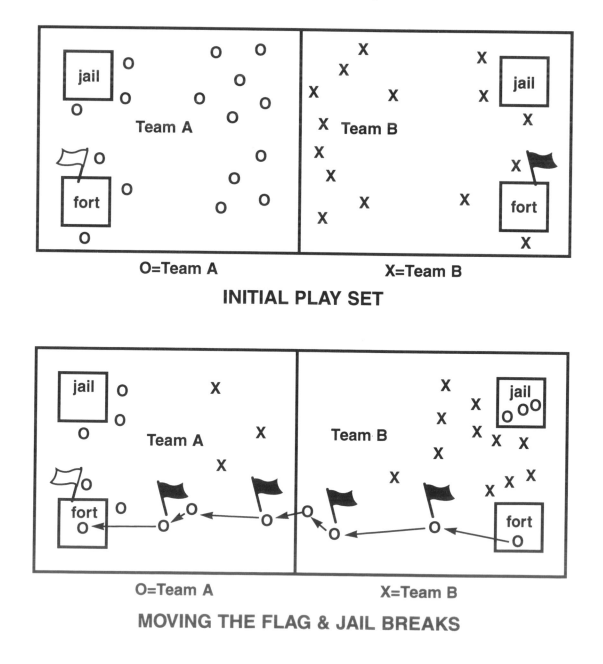

INITIAL PLAY SET

MOVING THE FLAG & JAIL BREAKS

Zlata's Diary:
A Child's Life in Sarajevo

by Zlata Filipovic
(Viking Penguin, 1994)

(Available in Canada, the United Kingdom, and Australia: Penguin)

Zlata's Diary is the actual diary of a young girl who was living in Sarajevo during the Bosnian War. At the age of eleven, Zlata began to keep a diary. In the beginning pages, she describes a happy life filled with holidays, birthday parties, and the beginning of a new school year. Within two months, she sees pictures on the television of bombings and fighting in nearby Dubrovnik. She feels concerned and scared for the people living there, but the reports are still distant and her life in Sarajevo has not changed. Five months later, Sarajevo is engulfed in war. There is no running water or electricity in the city. There is a shortage of food. Schools and public buildings are closed, and many have been destroyed by bombings. Shelling and sniper fire are a constant threat to anyone walking in the streets. Sarajevo is under constant siege. In her diary, Zlata describes the daily massacre that she sees happening outside her own window. She writes of her frustration and anger over losing her childhood and of her daily struggle for survival. Zlata's two-year diary is an honest account of survival under extreme wartime conditions.

Changing Borders

The borders of countries all over the world are constantly changing. New countries are founded, and old countries are usurped or absorbed. In some of the more volatile regions of the world, it is often difficult to keep up with who controls what countries and what the countries are called. One of the more recent areas of change has been in Eastern Europe. Since the end of the Cold War, ethnic diversity and the fight for democratic freedom have split many countries.

Compare the map below with one of Europe today. Make a list of the new countries that have come into existence since 1990. Choose one of the new countries and find out why it has changed names and who now controls the land.

Europe Pre-1990

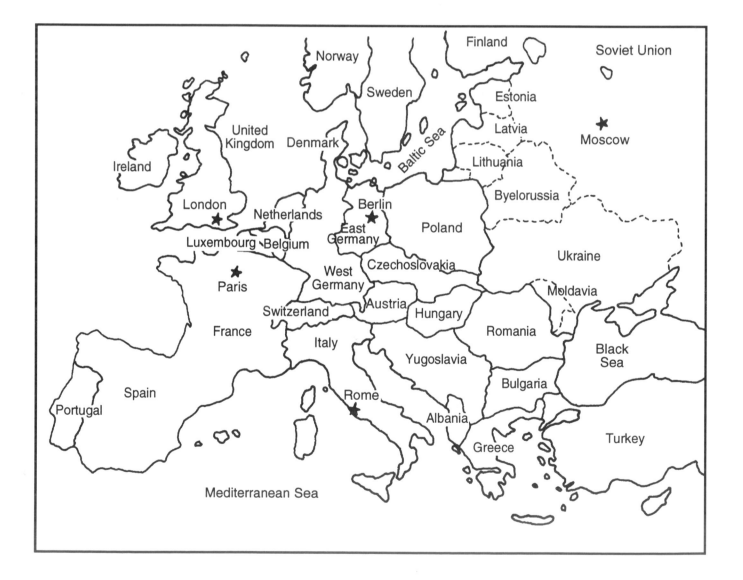

Name_____

Isolation

Although Zlata lived in a country across the Atlantic Ocean and thousands of miles away from the United States and Canada, she still enjoyed doing a lot of the same activities that Western teenagers enjoy. During the war, Zlata was unable to do any of these activities. She became depressed, bored, and lonely in her isolation.

Make a list of the activities that Zlata missed during the war and then make a list of the activities that you would miss if you were in her situation in your own house. Compare her list to your own. Are any of your ideas similar? What might you do to fill the endless hours of isolation?

Zlata's List	Your List

Name_____

Letters

Zlata received letters from friends and concerned students from all over the world. She read these letters over and over until she had memorized them. Why do you think these letters were so meaningful to Zlata?

_____

_____

_____

If you were to write a letter to a friend who was trapped in a war zone, what would you write to that friend? Use this space to draft a letter to your friend.

Name_____

UNICEF

UNICEF (United Nations International Children's Emergency Fund) was established in 1946. The agency's original mission was to help children who were living in European countries which had been devastated by war. Today, UNICEF has expanded its services and developed programs designed to serve children in need worldwide. In 1965, UNICEF was awarded the Nobel Peace Prize for its contributions.

Many of UNICEF's programs provide education and health care. The agency aids communities in improving sanitation, food quality, and water purity. In third world countries, UNICEF has established clinics which provide early pregnancy care and child immunizations as well as nutritional education. The agency's hope is that by educating the communities, the rate of mortality will decrease, and the quality of life will improve for all children.

UNICEF is overseen by a directing board with representatives from 44 different countries. The majority of the funding comes from government contributions. The remainder of the funding is supplied by private donations.

How did UNICEF help Zlata and her family?

_____

_____

_____

_____

_____

_____

_____

_____

_____

_____

_____

_____

_____

Research to find out more about UNICEF and the projects that the agency is currently directing. Share what you learn with the class.

Name_____

Before/After

Search the book for images which represent Zlata's life before and after March 5, 1992. Write these images in the Venn Diagram. Use these images to write one paragraph describing Zlata's life before the war started and one paragraph describing her life after the war took over her community. Then, participate in a class discussion based on what you have written.

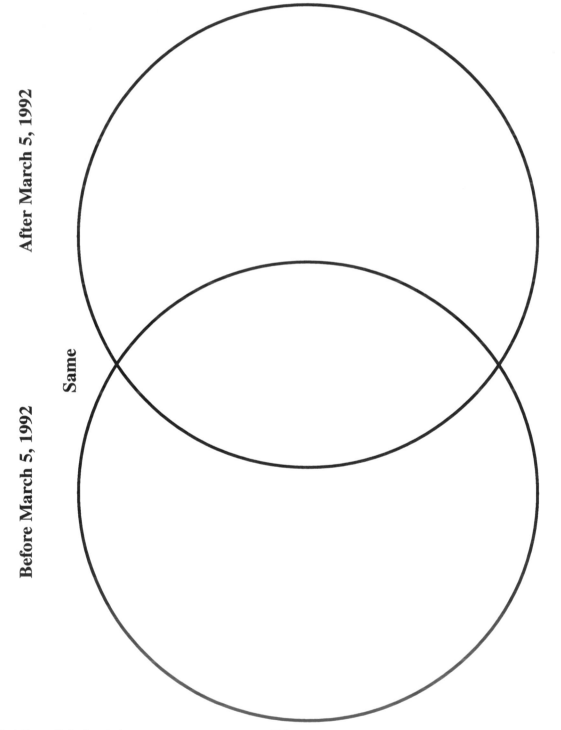

After March 5, 1992

Same

Before March 5, 1992

Name_____

People Are All the Same

On November 19, 1992, Zlata is once again frustrated with the political groups who have power. She does not understand why people have to fight. She writes, "But they are all people. They are all the same. They all look like people, there's no difference. They all have arms, legs and heads, they walk and talk, but now there's something that wants to make them different."

Do you agree with Zlata's statement? Are people all the same? Formulate an argument either for or against Zlata's statement. Be sure to support your argument with at least five facts. When complete, share your responses with your classmates.

_____

_____

_____

_____

_____

_____

_____

_____

_____

_____

_____

_____

_____

_____

_____

_____

_____

_____

_____

_____

_____

_____

Name _____

Politics

Politics is the art or science of making decisions which control and guide the government. Political decisions are made based on a government's philosophies or beliefs. This means that there is a set way of thinking and problem solving which is followed within the government. Every country has some form of political philosophy in effect within its ruling government. In the United States, there is a democratic system which allows every person in the country to have a say in how the country should be making decisions. Each citizen has the right to voice his/her opinion by voting. There are several other political philosophies which guide other societies around the world. Choose one of the following philosophies.

- Fascism
- Marxism
- Socialism
- National Communism
- Libertarianism
- Feudalism
- Democracy

Now, find out if and where the philosophy is being practiced today. Describe the beliefs behind the philosophy. Then, explain how a government adopting the philosophy would solve the following problems.

1. The leader of the government has just been found disposing of the food that has been stored for the winter months. _____

    _____

    _____

    _____

2. A neighboring country has threatened to invade one of the country's largest cities.

    _____

    _____

    _____

    _____

3. Several of the country's citizens are passing around a petition which states that the government is unfair.

    _____

    _____

    _____

    _____

Civil War

A civil war is one which takes place between two or more opposing groups of people who live in the same country. For example, the Civil War in the United States took place between the Union and the eleven southern states which attempted to secede, or split, from the Union in 1861. People on each side held different beliefs about slavery, finances, trade, and politics. The fight for opposing values led to a four-year war.

In *Zlata's Diary*, the civil war in Sarajevo is between the Croats, the Muslims, and the Serbs. In 1990, the Communist party freed Yugoslavia. This change in political control caused the evolution of a new government. The new political body was controlled by a democratically selected presidency board of Muslims, Croats, and Serbs. Although the three groups joined as members of the new presidency, they did not agree on several political issues. By 1991, the tension between these three ethnic groups, who were all vying for power and land, was so intense that war broke out among the three military powers. Unfortunately, as in most civil wars, there were hundreds of thousands of innocent civilians caught in the middle of the conflict.

Drawing from the information in *Zlata's Diary* and any supplemental information you can find in magazines, newspapers, or encyclopedias, draft a speech that you would deliver to the presidential board in Bosnia. In your speech, attempt to convince the panel that the civil war should stop. When you are finished, deliver your speech to the class and have a panel vote to decide whether your speech convinced them that the civil war in Bosnia should end.

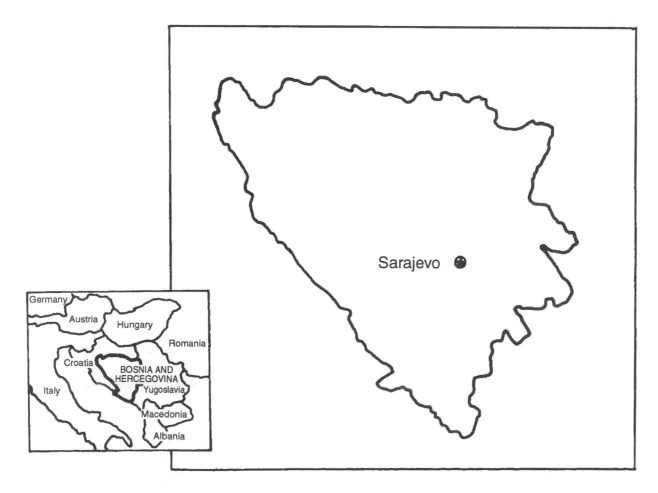

Name _____

Venting Emotions

Zlata's Diary is filled with words of anger, hope, sadness, and frustration. Throughout the war, she verbalized her emotions onto the pages of "Mimmy." One way we cope with difficult situations is to write down our feelings or to talk about them with a friend. Zlata's diary entries served the purpose as a form of therapy to help Zlata make sense of the war that was surrounding her. Think about a time when you were upset. Did writing or talking to someone help you feel better?

Make a list of all of the words you can think of that represent emotions.

Now, select words from your list that best describe Zlata's emotions when she wrote the following sentences.

1. "Life goes on. The past is cruel, that's exactly why we should forget it." _____

   _____

2. "... I want to scream and break everything!" _____

   _____

3. "The forces of war don't know anything about love and the desire to save something."_____

   _____

4. "...a child without a childhood." _____

   _____

5. "I read them and sometimes I cry, because I want them, I want life, not letters." _____

   _____

6. " Sometimes I think it would be better if they kept shooting, so that we wouldn't find it so hard when it starts up again...I am convinced now that it will never end."_____

   _____

7. " We haven't done anything. We're innocent. But helpless." _____

   _____

The Devil's Arithmetic

by Jane Yolen
(Viking Penguin, 1988)

(Available in Canada, the United Kingdom, and Australia: Penguin)

As modern-day Hannah opens the door of her great aunt's house, she looks out on a Polish village in the 1940s. When she turns back to question her family, she discovers everything has changed. She has been swept into the dream and is expected to play the role of a young girl named Chaya. She tries to convince everyone around her that she does not belong, but no one listens to her childish stories. When the Nazi soldiers arrive and begin to load the villagers into trucks for "relocation," Hannah realizes that she is now a victim and is going to be taken away to the concentration camps that her grandparents have spoken of so many times when remembering their lives as prisoners during WWII. She is terrified in her foreknowledge of the horrors that await her and the other villagers. Hannah is packed into a cattle car and is transported for four days with only one stop for water. When the train arrives at the camp, the people are brutally unloaded. Many dead are left behind in the car. Once at the camp, the people are forced to undress and shower. Their hair is shaved, they are deloused, and they are ultimately stripped of all humanity.

In the first day following her arrival at the camp, Hannah meets Rivka. Hannah learns the rules of camp survival from her new friend who has survived in the camp for over a year. From this day on, Hannah lives moment to moment. She survives by doing what is expected of her and by maintaining a sense of hope. One day, Hannah's friends are randomly "chosen." Hannah changes places with Rivka and bravely approaches her fate. As she steps through the door, she returns to her own time in history. Back in her aunt's house, Hannah has a better understanding and respect for what her great aunt and grandfather have endured in their quest for survival.

Name _____

Hunger and Thirst

When Hannah was transported in the train for four days, she and the other villagers were not given any food. During this time, the train made only one water stop for each of the boxcars. The water that the villagers received was filthy, but welcomed.

The Nazis knew that a healthy person can survive for only a couple of days without water, but he or she can survive several days without food. Without water, the body becomes dehydrated and can no longer perform its normal functions. The Nazis supplied the minimum that was required for survival.

In the concentration camp, the villagers received only a meager bowl of watery potato soup and sometimes a dried crust of bread. Hannah was fortunate to be selected to clean the charred cooking pots. In this job, she was able to scrape off and eat the burned pieces of potato that stuck to the bottoms of the pots. She was willing to eat anything for survival.

Think of a time when you were hot and thirsty after playing a sport on a summer day. How did your body feel before you were able to get a drink of water?

_____

_____

_____

_____

Remember a time when you missed or skipped a regular meal. How did your body react to the lack of food?

_____

_____

_____

Now imagine what it would be like if you had no control over when, what, and how much you could have to eat and drink. How would you feel?

_____

_____

_____

Discuss your answers to these questions with your classmates.

Name_____

Hope

The people living in the concentration camp live life moment to moment without any concept of the future. Every day, events occur which directly affect their chances for survival. Selections for "processing" are made randomly, food is minimal, work is demanding, and living conditions are abominable. Every moment of their lives, the prisoners are treated as subhuman and are forced to live in a state of uncertainty. The environment in the camp offers little motivation for survival.

Gilt indirectly discusses this issue with Hannah on the first night of their arrival in the camp. After Hannah's stomach grumbles loudly from lack of food, Gilt laughs aloud. Hannah is shocked by her behavior, and Gilt responds by saying, "Without laughter, there is no hope. Without hope, there is no life. Without life . . ." She does not complete the sentence. How do you think Gilt would have finished this sentence?

_____

_____

_____

_____

_____

_____

What does Gilt mean when she says, "Without hope, there is no life"? Do you agree with this statement?

_____

_____

_____

_____

_____

How do you think hope might have enhanced the prisoners' chances for survival?

_____

_____

_____

_____

Name_____

Rules for Survival

In the concentration camp, Rivka shares many rules of survival with Hannah and her friends. Below is a list of some of the survival rules that they discuss. Imagine that you are one of Hannah's friends. Read the rules and rank them in order of importance with regard to your own survival. (Place the ranking number on the line before the rule.) After ordering, justify each ranking.

_____ You must allow your friends to make their own survival decisions.

_____ You must learn which numbers belong to people who can organize things.

_____ You must memorize your own number.

_____ You must never go near the door to "Lilith's Cave."

_____ You must help the children hide in the midden.

_____ You must not think, just do what you are told.

_____ You must not ask the reason why.

_____ You must not lose your metal bowl.

Look through the novel and find other survival rules that are also observed in the camp. List them here and on the back.

_____

_____

_____

_____

_____

_____

_____

_____

_____

_____

_____

_____

_____

Name_____

Irony

Several times in the novel, the characters speak in cynical proverbs. The badchan frequently adopts this manner of speech in his role as the wedding entertainer. Through the irony of these statements, the reality of the situations is often more clearly identified.

Read the following quotes. Identify the speaker and explain the situation that he or she is implying or describing.

1. "The snake smiles but it shows no teeth."

   Speaker: _____

   Situation: _____

   _____

2. "Better the fox to guard the hen house and the wolves to guard the sheep."

   Speaker: _____

   Situation: _____

   _____

3. "God's hands are very hot and sweaty."

   Speaker: _____

   Situation: _____

   _____

4. "...a taker is not a giver. And a giver is not a taker either. Keep your thanks. And hand it on."

   Speaker: _____

   Situation: _____

   _____

5. "If you ask permission, the answer is no."

   Speaker: _____

   Situation: _____

   _____

6. "This is not a place for a fool, where there are idiots in charge."

   Speaker: _____

   Situation: _____

   _____

Name _____

Coping

When faced with an extreme survival situation, we all adapt and cope in our own ways. Some people give up and wait for death while others embrace life and strive to maintain it at all costs.

Explain how each of the following characters cope with the stresses and horrors of living in the concentration camp.

1. Hannah _____

_____

2. Gilt _____

_____

3. Schmuel _____

_____

4. Rivka _____

_____

5. Esther _____

_____

6. Shifre _____

_____

7. Fayge _____

_____

8. the badchan _____

_____

9. Tzipporah _____

_____

10. Leye _____

_____

11. the blokova _____

_____

Name_____

Euphemisms

A euphemism is an inoffensive word or phrase that is substituted for one that may be offensive or suggest something that is unpleasant. By using euphemisms, we often find it easier to discuss issues that may otherwise make us feel uncomfortable. Euphemisms are commonly used in our language today when we are referring to death. We sometimes say that someone has "passed away" or "gone to heaven" instead of using the more blunt and unpleasant word, "dead."

Leye explains that the Nazis use euphemisms as a way to deflect blame. If they do not verbalize and record death, then they feel there is no blame for death. Make a list of euphemisms from the novel. Beside each word or phrase, explain what the euphemism means.

Euphemism	Meaning

Extension:

On a separate paper, make a list of the euphemisms you have heard or used. Then answer, why do you or the people around you use these phrases?

Name_____

Holocaust

The word "holocaust" is commonly applied to any extensive human disaster. When capitalized, "Holocaust" is recognized as the massacre of Jews by the Nazis during WWII. Adolph Hitler believed that there should be only one pure race of German people and that Jews were inferior to this race. He ordered that all Jews should be annihilated. As a result, between 1939 and 1945 the Nazis systematically killed six million Jewish people.

Read the brief history of the Holocaust below. Use the space provided to do a freewrite on your thoughts. Share your ideas with your class.

Between 1933 and 1939, the Nazis gradually took away the business rights of the Jews. Jews were no longer allowed to own stores, and they could not receive any profits. This made it impossible for a family to survive. Financial upheaval was the first step of the Nazis' master plan.

When WWII started in 1939, the Nazis began to round up the Jews and place them into containment camps called ghettos. The Jews were forced to wear yellow stars, and they had few freedoms. In the ghettos, food was scarce and conditions were crowded, but families could stay together and some people were able to work. At this time, in an attempt to avoid imprisonment, many Jews fled the country or went into hiding. By 1942, the concentration camps, or death camps, were established. Jews were stripped of all belongings and were loaded into boxcars. The trains transported them to concentration camps located throughout Germany and Poland. In the concentration camps, the Nazis dehumanized and murdered millions of innocent men, women, and children.

Today, there are still reminders of the horrors of the Holocaust. Survivors still wear the numbers tattooed on their arms in the camps, and although the concentration camps were destroyed, the foundations of many of the buildings still exist.

Freewrite Response:

Name_____

Concentration Camp Map

Although the camp described in *The Devil's Arithmetic* is fictional, the facts about the camp are drawn from concentration camps which actually existed. Study the map below. (The political borders are set as they are recognized in 1994. Although some of the borders in this region have changed since 1945, the borders of the countries in which the camps were constructed are for the most part accurate.)

Locate the country in which each of the camps below was constructed.

- Auschwitz
- Belsen
- Belzig
- Buchenwald
- Chelmno
- Dachau
- Gross-Rosen
- Majdanek
- Mauthausen
- Neungamme
- Ravensbruck
- Sachsenhausen
- Sobibor
- Stutthof
- Treblinka

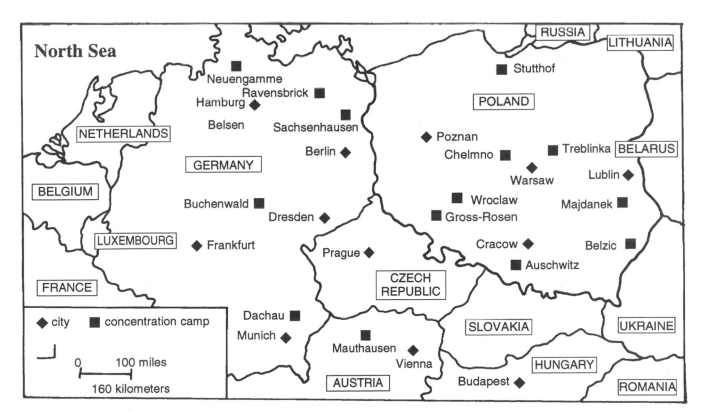

Where were most of the concentration camps located? Research to find out why this might be true.

Many of these camps had reputations during the war. Research to find out more about the different camps. Discuss what you learn with the class.

Name_____

"We Are All Heroes Here"

Hannah knows the fate of the Jews in the concentration camps. She realizes that six million will be killed before the end of the war, and she cannot comprehend how the people can passively allow the murders to happen. While working one day, she turns to Rivka and says, "We should go down fighting." She does not understand why the Jews do not fight for their human rights. Rivka disagrees. She points out that the Jews are weaponless and would stand little chance in a fight. She then recalls her mother's words telling her that it is more difficult to live and die in the concentration camp than it would be to die in a fight. She says that they are all heroes.

What does Rivka mean by the statement, "We are all heroes here"? Do you agree?

_____

_____

_____

_____

_____

_____

What are the traits of a hero? List at least five traits that you feel a hero must possess.

_____

_____

_____

_____

_____

Can these traits be applied to Rivka's and Hannah's characters?

_____

_____

_____

_____

_____

_____

Survival Theme Night or Camp Out

Camp Out

An ideal way to culminate your extended unit on survival would be to take your class on a camping trip to practice the survival skills they have learned in a real wilderness setting. If a camping trip is not a possibility, you may want to consider having a survival theme night at your school.

Survival Theme Night

A theme night can be an enjoyable way to close a unit. It is an especially good way to show off the students' hard work to their parents. An invitation can be found on page 171. Following is a suggested outline for how you might want to organize your theme night.

I. Student readings of survival stories or performances of survival skits

   Select stories or plays that your students have written during the unit to be read or performed for the parents.

II. Student projects and reports on display for viewing

   Set tables around the room with students' topographic maps, knots, survival kits, shelters, floating compass, notch calendar, animal tracks, and survival reports (page 172). Stories and flat maps can be displayed on classroom bulletin boards.

III. A ranger or other related specialist as a speaker

   Ask your students if any of their parents, aunts, uncles, or grandparents have worked as park rangers, search and rescue officials, fire persons, or any other survival-related occupations. (Grandparents are often wonderful resources to tap.) If not, call your local park and recreation department or chamber of commerce for resource suggestions.

IV. Refreshments

   Some refreshment suggestions and recipes are listed on page 170. These foods can be served in the coconut bowls that your students made during the island survival unit.

Food and Recipe Ideas

I. Food Suggestions

• dried fruit prepared by the class

• salted and/or dried meats

• dish prepared with a local wild plant (ex: fiddleheads, dandelion greens, etc.)

• biscuits with jam made by the class

• herb tea

II. Gorp

Ingredients:

1 c. (250 mL) raisins

1 c. (250 mL) peanuts

1 c. (250 mL) chocolate chips

Directions:

Pour ingredients together in a bag. This recipe serves six.

III. Coconut Macaroons

Ingredients:

3 egg whites

1½ c. (375 mL) shredded coconut (from shell bowl activity, page 109)

⅛ tsp. (.75 mL) salt

¾ c. (185 mL) sugar

¼ tsp. (1.5 mL) vanilla

Directions:

Shred chunked coconut in a food processor and then soak in coconut milk for a few hours to moisten. Beat the egg whites, vanilla, and salt until light and foamy. Slowly beat in the sugar. Fold in the coconut. Drop by teaspoons onto a greased cookie sheet. Bake at 300°F (150°C) for 20 minutes or until browned. This recipe yields about two dozen cookies.

You are invited to
Survival Theme Night

Where: _____

Date: _____

Time: _____

Given by: _____

Report Guidelines

Choose a topic concerning survival which interests you and which your class did not discuss extensively. Get approval for your topic from your teacher. Then, write and present a survival report. Use the following guidelines to help you organize your report.

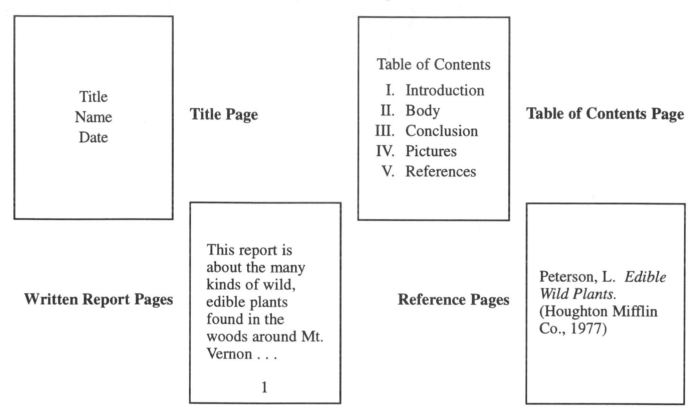

Title Page: Write the title, your name, and the date on the cover page of your report.

Table of Contents: The table of contents is an outline of your report.

    I. Introduction: Your report should begin with an introduction. In this paragraph you want to explain what your report is about. It is also important to provide your reader with any background information he/she might need to understand your topic.

    II. Body: This portion of your report is the information center. The body should consist of several paragraphs presenting your ideas. (You can outline these ideas in the table of contents next to Roman numeral II.)

    III. Conclusion: The conclusion is the final paragraph of your report. In this paragraph you should briefly restate what your report was about.

    IV. Pictures/Diagrams: It is often helpful to include pictures or diagrams to explain your information further.

    V. References: The final page of your report should include a list of the books that you used to write your report.

Written Report: The written report should have several paragraphs presenting your information. The writing should be clear and well organized. Follow any additional guidelines about organization that your teacher may require.

References: Your references should be listed in alphabetical order by the authors' last names.

Survival Skill Master

You're on the right track!

To: _____

For: _____

Teacher: _____

Date: _____

Answer Key

Page 9: Survival Scramble

1. shelter
2. instinct
3. prepared
4. water
5. survey
6. food
7. clothing

A person must have *courage* for survival.

Page 18: Rationing

Answers	Challenge	
eggs	done	1.14, 1.71
sandwiches	7.14, 10.71	2.38, 3.57
candy	1.71, 2.56	0.57, 0.85
chips	0.86, 1.29	0.28, 0.43
bagels	3.71, 5.57	1.23, 1.86
oranges	2.57, 3.86	0.86, 1.29
apples	1.14, 1.71	0.38, 0.57
water	2.00, 3.00	0.67, 1.00

Page 26: Tree and Plant Wordsearch

Page 28: Animal Tracking

1. fox
2. deer
3. rabbit
4. mink
5. mouse
6. skunk
7. squirrel
8. raccoon

Page 29: Animal Survival Instincts

1. crocodile
2. firefly
3. wolf
4. crow
5. fawn
6. kitten
7. swallow
8. turkey
9. bee
10. monkey

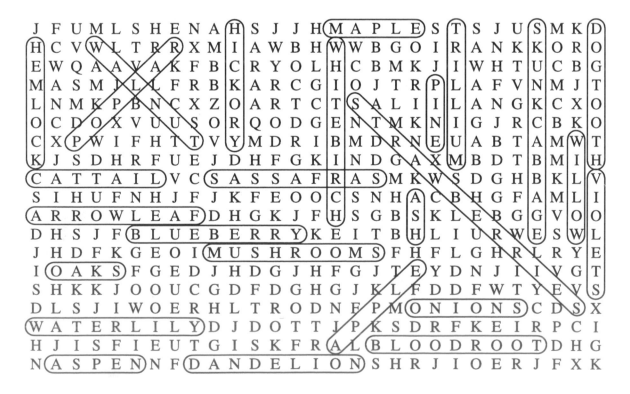

Answer Key (cont.)

Page 35: Nutritional Number Facts

1. proteins
2. carbohydrates
3. fats
4. minerals
5. vitamins
6. water

Page 45: Graphing Food

1. 25 cups
2. 55 cups
3. 10 quarts
4. 20 cups
5. 10 pints
6. 23 cups
7. skunk cabbage
8. mushrooms
9. 12 ½ cups

1. 5 pounds
2. 320 ounces
3. 10 pounds
4. 13 ½ pounds
5. 110 pounds

Page 47: Math in the Catskills

1. a. 62" or 157 cm
   b. 5" or 12.5 cm
2. a. 240 quarts or 228 liters
   b. 24 jars
3. a. July 22
   b. 192
4. a. ¾ hour
   b. 10 ⅔ miles or 17.06 km

Page 52: Donn's Trail Map

1. 4–5 miles, 6.4–8 km
2. twice
3. Wassataquoik Stream
4. B, 2
5. south
6. Answers will vary.
7. setting sun

Page 71: Temperature Conversions

A. 1. –90°F
   2. –85°F
B. 1. –10°C to –4.4°C
   2. –27.2°C to –13°C
   3. –28.9°C to –18.9°C
   4. –15.6°C to –3.3°C
   5. –6.7°C to 0°C

Page 72: True North

1. Alaska 35
2. Indiana, Kentucky, Tennessee, Georgia, Florida, Wisconsin 0

Page 106: Sea Measurement

1. 2 hours and 5 minutes
2. 4 hours to 7 hours and 40 minutes
3. 18 feet or 5.4 meters
4. 48 feet or 14.4 meters deep
5. 20 knots
6. 10 knots

Page 107: Longitude and Latitude

1. 3,330 km
2. 7,824 km
3. 8,325 km
4. 6,660 km
5. 39,960 km
6. Answers will differ.

Answer Key *(cont.)*

Page 121: Translation Puzzle

Across

1. Temori
2. Puaa
3. Kivi
4. Maui
5. Fei
6. Mafatu
7. Smoking Islands
8. Hikueru
9. Uri
10. Moan
11. Mape

Down

1. Tavananui
2. Pahua
3. Aramoana
4. Marae
5. Feke
6. Pareu
7. Tupapau
8. Motutabu

Page 144: Percentages

Dairy 25%
Grains 17%
Fruits 10%
Vegetables 23 %
Meats 18 %
Fats 7%

Page 145: Roadblock Logic

1. 2nd, A, 3rd, C, 4th
   2nd, B, 3rd, C, 4th
   2nd, B, 1st, D, 2nd, C, 4th
2. 3rd, B, 1st
3. 3rd, B, 2nd, A
4. 4
5. 4
6. 3rd, B
7. B, 3rd, C, 2nd, D, 1st
   B, 3rd, A, 2nd, B, 1st
   B, 1st
   B, 3rd, A, 2nd, C, 1st
   B, 2nd, C, 1st
8. Hannah - 3rd, C, 4th
   Tom - B, 3rd, C, 4th